The

I Love To Write

Book

The

I Love To Write

Book

IDEAS & TIPS
FOR YOUNG WRITERS

by
Mary-Lane Kamberg

preface by
John Riddle
Founder of I Love To Write Day

CRICKHOLLOW BOOKS

Crickhollow Books is an imprint of Great Lakes Literary, LLC, of Milwaukee, Wisconsin, an independent press working to create books of lasting quality and practical value.

Our titles are available from your favorite bookstore or your favorite library jobber or wholesale vendor.

For a complete catalog of all our titles or to place special orders, visit our website: www.CrickhollowBooks.com

The I Love To Write Book
© 2008, Mary-Lane Kamberg

FOR EACH BOOK SOLD, a donation will be made to the I Love To Write Day project, a nonprofit organization working to encourage more enthusiasm for writing across the United States. Crickhollow Books has no direct affiliation with that organization but strongly endorses its mission: to get more people of all ages writing and enjoying it!

Publisher's Cataloging-In-Publication Data
(Prepared by The Donohue Group, Inc.)

Kamberg, Mary-Lane, 1948–
   The I Love To Write book : ideas & tips for young writers / by Mary-Lane Kamberg ; preface by John Riddle. – 1st ed.

   p. ; cm.

   Includes index.
   Published in support of "I Love To Write Day."
   ISBN: 978-1-933987-05-7

1. English language – Composition and exercises.   2. Composition (Language Arts) – Study and teaching – Activity programs.   I. Riddle, John. II. Title.

PE1413 K2 2008
808.042

First Edition • Original Trade Paperback
10 9 8 7 6 5 4 3 2 1

More information

For more, visit the website for *The I Love to Write Book*
www.lovetowritebook.org

to find basic information, advanced tips, a place to ask questions
about anything in this book and other writing topics,
success stories of young writers, interviews about writing
with some of your favorite writers . . .
plus the occasional contest
and other fun stuff!

For Audrey and Clayton Phillips

Acknowledgements

Thanks go to those who have encouraged my writer's journey and who have helped with this book: Molly Brown, my first reader; the late Wilma Yeo for inviting me to join the Kansas City Writers Group, where I continue to learn to write; Teresa Fink for her last-minute help; Keith Johnson, of *Johnson's County Gazette*, who published my first freelance work; Robert C. Jones, my poetry mentor; Lois Daniel for teaching me how to sell my work; Chalise Bourque for editorial support; Sophia Myers for her encouragement; and the Warrensburg Writers Circle, Kansas City Writers Group, and the Kansas City Young Writers Camp.

Thanks, too, to Carol Hamilton, Emily Hendricks, Sally Jadlow, Judith Bader Jones, Frank Parman, Janet Sunderland, for research assistance and contributors Harris Bailey, Thomas Fink, Matara Hitchcock, Julia Marquez, Terry Hoyland, Audrey Phillips, Clayton Phillips, Polly Swafford, and Becca Zeiger.

I also thank my husband Ken Kamberg, my mother and No. 1 fan Jessie Ladewig, my daughters Rebekka and Johanna, and my supportive extended family.

Finally, thanks to my publisher Philip Martin and my agents Mike and Susan Farris of Farris Literary Agency.

"To learn the act of writing
is to obtain magical powers.
They are a secret.
No one can give them to
you. You must work at them
yourself."
Natalie Goldberg (1948–),
creative-writing teacher and author
of *Writing Down the Bones*

Credits

The following poems previously appeared in the following publications:

"My Grandmother," by Mary-Lane Kamberg, in *Potpourri*

"checking out," by Polly Swafford, in *Kansas City Writers Group Holiday Collection*

"fat robin," by Polly Swafford, in *Mid-America Poetry Review*

"first snowfall," by Polly Swafford, in *ByLine*

"bedtime –" by Polly Swafford, in *Kansas City Star*

"black birds chatter," by Polly Swafford, in *Kansas City Star*

"soft snowflakes," by Polly Swafford, in *Kansas City Star*

Preface

About the Origins of "I Love To Write Day"

by John Riddle, Founder

In the spring of 2002, I was driving from my home in Delaware to the Blue Ridge Mountain Christian Writer's conference in Asheville, North Carolina, where I was scheduled to speak. My oldest daughter, Bonnie, was in the car with me; she was a college student at the time and wanted to attend some of the workshops. Even though she was already a published writer, she knew the value of learning more about the craft of writing.

Passing through the Richmond, Virginia, area, I was thinking about a magazine interview I had to do the next week. Normally I am the one interviewing someone else for an article, but this time I was going to be the subject of the piece. *Writer's Digest* magazine wanted to do a profile of me, highlighting my success in writing for many websites over the past months.

A little background: when I worked in the fundraising field, years ago, I loved planning big special events. Once I tried to get a record into the *Guinness Book of World Records* by having the largest number of people dance the "Twist" in one location. I even got Chubby Checker to tape some public service announcements to help promote the event.

Now, as I drove through Richmond – as a writer and author, I knew I needed a website – I came up with the name I Love To Write.com (now evolved into http://www.ilovetowriteday.org). It didn't take long to develop that a bit further into the idea of holding the "world's largest party for writers."

I remember telling Bonnie to remember this moment, when I "officially declared" November 15 to be I Love To Write Day. I knew in my heart that the I Love To Write Day event would be a success.

However, never in my wildest dreams did I believe how successful it would become! Two weeks after the Blue Ridge Mountain conference was over, I established the I Love To Write Day website and began to send out press releases to media outlets all across the United States. I also sent information to schools, bookstores, and libraries.

About ten days later, I started getting numerous media requests for interviews and more info about I Love To Write Day. And the response from schools was absolutely overwhelming. By the time November 15, 2002, rolled around, more than 11,000 schools all across the country had signed up to hold special I Love To Write Day events and activities. Bookstores, libraries, churches, community centers and even a few malls joined in the fun. When *USA Today* published an interview with me about the first year's event, my phone didn't stop ringing, and I lost track of how many e-mails I was receiving.

As of this writing, the governors of nine states have officially proclaimed November 15 as I Love To Write Day in their states, urging all of their residents to find time to write and celebrate the day.

My goal for I Love To Write Day is simple: people of all ages are encouraged to write something. A poem, a letter, an essay, start a novel, finish a novel . . . the possibilities are endless!

Hundreds of people e-mailed or wrote to me shortly after the first I Love To Write Day. They shared samples of what they had written, and told how they enjoyed writing again.

Unfortunately, too many people don't write or don't seem to enjoy writing. For them, the thought of putting words on a piece of paper (or a computer screen) can be a frightening experience.

I encourage everyone to remember how important writing can be. Spend some time writing something today! You don't have to set a goal of writing a novel (unless you have wanted to write one for a long time); just write something that is short, and meaningful to you.

Writing can be fun, but it is also challenging. I believe that people need to be challenged, and writing is one of many creative ways to express yourself.

I am very excited because each year, more I Love To Write Day activities are planned all across the United States. For some, that will be the beginning of a writing career.

I Love To Write Day has the potential to launch the career of the next John Grisham, Mary Higgins Clark, Stephen King or Toni Morrison.

For young writers, it can help develop the next J.K. Rowling or other very famous, successful, and beloved writer.

I encourage you to visit the official I Love To Write Day website. The web address is www.ilovetowriteday.org. Visit today to learn how you can join in the fun.

When people become stronger writers, they become better communicators . . . and everyone wins!

August 7, 2008

John Riddle, Founder
I Love To Write Day
www.ilovetowriteday.org

Contents

SECTION III: REVISE, EDIT, AND PROOFREAD

Get Started

Were You Born To Write?

Even the earliest groups of humans told stories. They sat around cooking fires and told stories about their travels, hunts, and fights. Some storytellers made up their stories.

Today, storytellers are everywhere. Your teachers use stories to help you learn. You and your friends tell stories just for fun. A favorite relative talks about the good old days.

Some storytellers earn money from their stories. They work for newspapers, radio and television stations, movie producers, advertising agencies, book publishers, and other companies. Or, they work for themselves.

They are *writers*.

Perhaps you've wondered . . . could I be a *writer?*

The answer, of course, is *YES!*

> "A writer is someone who writes, that's all. You can't stop it; you can't make yourself do anything else but that."
>
> Gore Vidal (1925–), American novelist, playwright, and essayist. His first novel was published when he was 21.

What Are Writers Like?

Writers have many different life experiences. They like different activities. They have different tastes in music. And like different foods.

But writers share some interesting characteristics.

On the next page, you'll find a list of typical characteristics of a writer.

Am I a Writer?

Make a checkmark next to the ones that describe you, too:

___ 1. I am curious.

___ 2. I like to know what's happening.

___ 3. I like to be with other people.

___ 4. I like spending time alone.

___ 5 I like to read everything: books, newspapers, even the backs of cereal boxes.

___ 6. I love school supplies, especially new notebooks and pens.

___ 7. I like to watch television and go to movies.

___ 8. I like to listen to other people's conversations.

___ 9. I am nosey.

___ 10. I like word games (like hangman, crossword puzzles, word jumbles, word searches).

___ 11. I am sensitive.

___ 12. I like e-mail.

___ 13. I wonder why people do the things they do.

___ 14. I like gossip.

___ 15. I write.

___ 16. I like to watch what people do.

___ 17. I like to observe my surroundings.

___ 18. I have a good imagination.

___ 19. I think a lot.

___ 20. I often daydream.

Count the number of checks you made. The more items you checked, the more you are like other writers.

But one thing above is more important than the others. If you checked "I write," you *are* a writer!

MARY-LANE KAMBERG

And if you're a writer, you *have* to write. (You just can't help it!)

Not all writers publish their work. But if you'd like to see your work in print, the key is to improve your skills.

You'll learn about getting published in Section III (see pages 115–123).

What if . . . You're Not a Born Writer?

You might not be a born writer.

But you might become one after all, even if you don't start out planning to be a writer.

There are many other jobs that require writing skills!

"I know that I'm a real writer because sometimes I write a story just because I want to; not because someone's told me to."

Fay Weldon (1931–), English writer; her books for children include *Wolf the Mechanical Dog, Party Puddle,* and *Nobody Likes Me*

⇨ **Try this!**

Match the following occupations with writing activities that people in these jobs perform (see answers on page 127):

__ Police officer	a. notes to kid's teachers
__ Sales manager	b. results of experiments
__ Senator	c. memos to employees
__ Medical examiner	d. lawsuits
__ Fire marshal	e. sales reports
__ Scientist	f. traffic accident reports
__ Business owner	g. report of a fire investigation
__ Parent	h. new laws
__ Lawyer	i. autopsy reports

What jobs that need writers can you add to this list?

_____

_____

Worksheet: My Profile as a Writer

What have you written recently (letters, poems, journal entries, school assignments, newspaper articles . . .)?

_____

_____

_____

_____

What would you most like to write sometime soon?

_____

_____

_____

_____

What career do you have in mind?

_____

_____

What will you need to write if you work in that job?

_____

_____

What do you think are your best writing-related skills?

_____

_____

What writing skills would you like to improve?

_____

_____

_____

Read, Read, Read

The more you read, the better you will write.

When you read good books, poems, or magazine articles, do you ever think about how the writer learned to write so well? Do you wonder what you could do to write like that?

The easiest way to learn to write is to read. Read books, magazines, newspaper articles, comic books, and signs on the subway. Read just for fun! When you read, you are learning how to write.

Here are some tips for readers who also want to be writers:

> "You really ought to read more books.
> You know, those things that look like blocks but come apart on one side."
>
> F. Scott Fitzgerald (1896–1940), American novelist and short-story writer, best known for *The Great Gatsby*

1. Read what you want to write.

If you were going to write a book, what kind of book would it be? That's just the kind of books you should read.

If you want to write mysteries, read mysteries. If you want to write fantasies, read fantasies. If you want to write true stories, read newspapers, magazines, and nonfiction books.

By reading your favorite kind of book, you'll become an expert in that type of book. You'll see what other writers do to make you like their books.

In a mystery, for instance, you'll notice that the character who commits the crime is introduced early in the story. When you get ready to write your own mystery, you'll sneak the criminal into the early pages of the story. You'll do it without thinking about it, because you'll be so used to the way mystery writers tell stories.

2. Read other stuff.

You can also learn to write better mysteries by reading different types of books. If you usually read novels, ask your librarian for a book about baseball, the Civil War, or aircraft. If you usually read fantasy, pick up a book of poems. The more different types of books you read, the better your writing will become – even if you never write those types of stories.

▶ *Definition: Genre*

Genre is the category a work falls into. In literature, genre means categories like novel, poem, or essay. It also refers to more specific categories like mystery, comedy, Western, science fiction, or horror. Genre also applies to such other art forms as music (classical, hip hop, country, rock and roll) and visual art (landscape, portrait, folk art, cartoon).

3. Read as a writer.

When you read, read as a writer. Pay attention to how the author uses words. See if you can figure out why the writer used one word instead of another.

If you feel sad after reading a paragraph or chapter, look back at what you just read. Why did you feel that way? Did you care about the characters? What made you care? What else did the writer do to get you running for a tissue?

If you laugh at part of a book, figure out what made it funny. Was it something a character said? Was it a vocabulary word or some action? Was it an element of surprise that made you smile?

The more you read, the more you'll gain a sense of how to tell stories.

⇨ **Try this!**

Find a part in a book that makes you sad, or happy, or worried. See if you can tell how the writer helped you feel that emotion.

Now try to write a couple of paragraphs that imitate the writer's style. Can you use some of the same tricks to make a reader cry? Or laugh? Or feel suspense?

On the Hunt for Ideas

If you're on the lookout for ideas to write about, hunt where other writers stalk their prey. Ideas are everywhere, but sometimes they're hard to see.

Have you noticed the way a drop of water holds onto the bottom of a leaf after a rainfall? That is a wonderful image to write about!

Did you have a fight with your brother or sister because you wanted to watch different television shows? That conflict is a good story starter!

What did you learn in science class that you'd like to know more about? Search the Internet and write a report.

Whenever you get a writing idea, write it down and put it in an "Idea Keeper." Your Idea Keeper can be a notebook, or a special box, file folder, or basket of index cards where you jot down notes about something you saw, heard, felt, tasted, smelled, thought about, or imagined.

Whichever Idea Keeper you choose, always carry some sort of notebook with you. That way, when you get a writing idea, you can write it down quickly and save it for later.

> "Everybody walks past a thousand story ideas every day. The good writers are the ones who see five or six of them. Most people don't see any."
>
> Orson Scott Card (1951–), American science-fiction writer, author of *Ender's Game*, *Ender's Shadow*, and *Speaker for the Dead*

Ask "What if...?"

One way that writers come up with ideas for writing is to ask *What if...?* Take a look at the list below and see which ones interest you. Choose one to write about:

What if your teacher were an undercover detective?

What if you were born during the Revolutionary War? Which side would you fight for?

What if you climbed a mountain and found a secret village at the top?

What if you rode a horse to school?

What if there were one bear and three little girls?

What if you found a key in your attic and later found a locked drawer in a desk in the basement?

What if you found a sack of money buried in your grandmother's garden?

What if you could read your best friend's mind?

What if you worked as a roadie for your favorite band?

What if you found a secret cave in the woods?

What if all your friends were invited to a birthday party – except you?

What if you had to warn the whole neighborhood about a pack of wild dogs?

What if you got what you wanted for your birthday? What if you didn't?

What if you lost something important to you? What if your best friend stole it?

Add your own " What if . . . ?":

_____

_____

_____

➡ **Try this!**

Make an Idea Keeper.

An Idea Keeper is a notebook or other place where you can jot down notes about writing ideas or observations, things you saw or heard. . . .

Take it and a pen or pencil with you everywhere you go for one week. When you notice something interesting, write it down. It might be something you see, something that bothers you, or something exciting that happens. At the end of the week, write about one of the things in your notebook.

MARY-LANE KAMBERG

Write about People, Places, and Things

Write about people, places, and things. Write from your own experience.

Or, start writing about something that happened, but stop part-way and ask *What if...?*

Change actual events to what might have happened if something had been different. Write from your imagination.

Make up people and write about them. Give them names. Place them in your hometown or somewhere you went on vacation.

Invent objects for them to use.

Below and on the next pages, you'll find some writing ideas to get you started:

People

Someone famous
Your next-door neighbor
Your grandfather
Your grandmother
A waitress
Your doctor
Your cousin
Someone who taught you something
Your best friend
Someone you would like to be
Someone you feel sorry for
Someone who is good at math
Someone with a job you'd like

Add your own:

_____

_____

_____

Places

Your bedroom
A sunny place
Somewhere cold
A school
A place you went on vacation
A garden
A basement
An attic
A stairway
A lake
A playground
Your grandmother's kitchen
A beach
A mountain
A forest
Somewhere to hide
A parking lot
A zoo
A shopping mall
A theater
A secret door
A desert
A creek
A museum

Add your own:

_____

_____

_____

MARY-LANE KAMBERG

Things

A statue
A song
A stuffed animal
A letter
A photograph or painting
A musical instrument
A book
Something you bought
Something you wish you had
Your father's favorite chair
Something you lost
Your pet
Your mother's jewelry
Something you got in the mail
A tree house
A skateboard
A ghost
A space alien
An underwater city
A boat
A bicycle
A car or truck
Hair
Your favorite class
Your favorite season
A favorite toy
Treasures

Add your own:

_____

_____

_____

Write from your own real (or imagined) experiences.

The best (or worst) party you attended
A bus ride
A vacation
The first (or last) day of school
The birth (or death) of a person or pet
Something you learned
A problem you (or someone else) solved
Fishing
A time you cooked something
Camping
Swimming
Horseback riding
A dance recital
Walking to school
Making a mistake
A trip to outer space
A fight you had with a friend
A thunderstorm or blizzard

Add your own:

_____

_____

_____

⇨ **Try this!**

Choose a *What if...?* from the list above. Then choose one item from each of the three lists of persons, places, and things.

Now, write a story about the *What if...?* that includes all three items.

⇨ **Try this!**

Make up your own *What if...?*.

Write a paragraph about it.

MARY-LANE KAMBERG

Write for Ideas

Sometimes writers do what is called "free writing" to get their ideas flowing. They start by putting pen to paper and making their hands move, writing anything and everything that comes into their minds. And when something they've written reminds them of something else, they write about that, too.

Here's an example of a poem that started just this way.

No Idea What To Write!

I have no idea what to write!
Will I write about a kite?
Kitties and yarn, dogs and a bone?
UFOs, aliens, and their clone?
Goblins and flying bats?
Scary witches and their cats?
A big hot sun and some beaches,
With no more lessons a teacher teaches?
Pirates that have you walk the plank?
Loads of fish in their tank?
What about a ship that sank?
Why is my mind still drawing a blank?
Famous explorers without a map?
Falling into a native trap?
A Superman without a cape,
Stolen by a hungry ape?
How ever can he escape?
What about highway traffic?
Someone who is photogenic?
Now I look in front of me,
And what do my brown eyes see?
A big long page of poetry!

— Matara Hitchcock, 4th grade

"There is nothing to write about, you say.

Well then, write and let me know just this – that there is nothing to write about."

Pliny the Younger (61–112 A.D.) Roman senator and author. His letters are an important source of Roman history.

✔ Writing Tip

Try "free writing." What's that?

Here's a method described by Natalie Goldberg in her book of tips for writers, *Writing Down the Bones*:

- Set a timer for 10 or 15 minutes.
  The amount of time doesn't matter. Promise yourself that you will write until the timer goes off.
- *Go!*
- Write as fast as you can. Keep your pen or pencil moving so fast you have no time to think about what you're writing.
- Ignore everything around you: the stereo, the sound of your sister playing a video game, your cat meowing to go outside.
- Write without stopping . . . even if you can't think of anything to say! (If that happens, just write, "I am practicing writing. I am practicing writing…" until something comes to mind.)
- Ignore grammar, spelling, and punctuation. They'll slow you down. You can make corrections later.
- If you make a mistake, keep going. Leave it and write what you meant to write next to it. (Crossing out slows you down.)
- Write whatever comes into your head. If that reminds you of something else, write about that, too.
- Keep writing until the timer rings.

When you finish free-writing, read what you wrote without criticizing yourself or your writing. Your writing might be fantastic, or it might be a bunch of stupid stuff that makes no sense at all. It makes no difference. Somewhere in what you have written is an idea – probably several ideas. Write about them now, or put them in your Idea Keeper.

If you're ever stuck for an idea, look in your Idea Keeper, read your free-writing notebook pages, or free-write again.

MARY-LANE KAMBERG

Observe the World

An important skill all writers need is the ability to notice things. You probably already have good observation skills. But you can always improve them.

Observation is important because the more details you add to your writing, the stronger it will be.

The two main areas writers pay attention to are their surroundings and the people around them.

Look around the room. Look out the window. When you go somewhere – the drugstore, your grandma's house, the Grand Canyon – what do you notice? The ability to describe the world starts with paying attention to significant details . . . for example, a wisp of white across the sky, or a chipmunk missing a chunk out of its ear.

Because humans experience the world through the senses, the first step is to observe the sights, smells, tastes, sounds, and textures. Simply "notice" them. The second step is to write them down in your Idea Keeper or a journal you take with you wherever you go. You may never use some of the details you record. That's okay. Writing them down increases your observation skills. And chances are you will use at least some of them in something you write.

> "We shall not cease from exploration, and the end of all our exploring will be to arrive where we started and know the place for the first time."

T. S. Eliot (1888–1965), American poet and winner of the 1948 Nobel Prize in Literature.

Notice the landscape

Wherever you are, observe your landscape from top to bottom and from left to right. Start with the sky: what color is it? Are there clouds? What kind? What color? What do they look like? What else do you see in the sky? Airplanes? Birds? UFOs? The sun? The moon?

Now look at the bottom of the picture. Is it ground or water? If ground, is it farmland or mountains? Does the farm have a name? The Quarter-Mile Farm? What mountain range is it? The Adirondacks? If you see water, is it an ocean, lake, river, creek? What is its official name?

The Pacific Ocean? The Grand Lake of the Cherokees? The Hudson River? Jack's Defeat Creek?

What's between the sky and the ground or the water? Start at the left and look to the right. Are there buildings? Boats? What kind? How big? What colors do you see? Are there plants? What are their names? Oaks? Palm trees? Grape vines? Cornstalks? What about animals? Cows? Giraffes? Polar bears?

✔ Writing Tip

One way to create the look and feeling of a setting is to focus on the season. If it's winter, for example, use cold words throughout your story, like *dark, drab, frigid, black, damp, wet, stark, empty, ice, snow,* and *storm.* If it's summer, use words like *light, warm, hot, breezy, shade, rain, blue, green,* and *dry.*

Another kind of observation is watching people. For this, just look and listen. How does the person walk? Does she limp? Does he bounce along the sidewalk? When she moves, is she slow and deliberate? Or does she rush through her day?

How does the person talk? Does his accent reveal he's from the South? Or a foreign country? Does she stammer or have a lisp? How does someone show that she is listening – or not listening – to another?

Use traits you observe in real people to describe the characters in your poems and stories.

These are the kinds of details that enrich your writing. The more specific you are, the better. When you show your old, young, rich, poor, scared, or confident characters moving through schools, fields, airports, or forests, readers better understand the people you create.

Make connections

Another part of observing is to make connections between things that you notice, especially things that seem out of place.

For example, if you're at a Civil War re-enactment where costumed actors are fighting a battle, suppose you notice one of the "soldiers," dressed in a Union uniform, on a cell phone. Those two things usually don't go together! Jot that down in your notebook. You might later use those images in a science-fiction story . . . or a short poem like this:

Civil War Re-enactment

smoke and cannonballs —
Union soldier
talks on cell phone

> *— Mary-Lane Kamberg*

Create a setting

When you write stories, poems, history reports, newspaper articles, or other types of writing, enrich your readers' experience. Show them the setting where the events occur.

Start by answering the question, *Where does my story take place?*

✔ Writing Tip

For a true story, use your observations of the actual place the action happened. In a fictional story or poem, use details drawn from your imagination – or from your own experience with something similar (look in your Idea Keeper for ideas).

The key to creating a memorable setting lies in *details:* the ones you include . . . and the ones you leave out.

Create a mood by selecting *only* those details of the landscape that contribute to the mood.

For example, if your setting is a pond in a city park, you might observe a swan swimming, a lunch sack floating on the water, children playing tag, a baby crying, a tree broken in two by lightning, blooming roses. (Write them all down!)

Then, if you want to create a happy mood, you might choose to show the reader the swan, the children playing tag, the blooming roses. If you want to create a bad mood, you might choose to show the crying baby, the broken tree, the trash floating on the water.

(That's why you want to take as many notes as you can of many different items. The more you have to choose from, the better your choices will be and the less you'll have to imagine.)

The same goes for the people in the story. If you are writing about real people, include gestures they use, and ways they walk and talk. A man might point to emphasize what he says. A child walks with a different posture if she is sad or happy. If you are writing about fictional characters, include some gestures and postures you've observed by watching real people.

 Try this!

Take a notebook wherever you go. Make lists of sights, sounds, tastes, smells, textures. Record what you see. A pop that sounds like gunfire. A little girl crying. The smell of bacon frying before you leave your bedroom on your birthday morning.

 Try this!

Take a pencil and notebook with you to a park. While you're there, write down everything you see, smell, hear, taste, and touch. (You might have to actually touch the tree bark or the concrete park-bench.)

At home, separate the images into one list of things a sad person might notice and one list of things a happy person might notice.

Write a poem or paragraph about a person who is sad – using some of the items on the "sad" list. Write another poem or paragraph about someone who is happy – using some of the items on the "happy" list.

 Try this!

Write a paragraph that describes your hometown. Give examples of things you see, hear, smell, taste, and touch. What does your town look like? What sounds do you hear on a moonless summer night? Does a river run through town? What kinds of trees, bushes, or other plants grow there?

What foods are most popular or unique in your town?

What smells are common? Ocean air? Lilac bushes?

Grand Openings

No matter what you're writing, you want your first line to grab readers by the throat and drag them into your story.

Surprisingly, if you're writing fiction, the worst place to start a story is at the beginning.

That's right. The worst place to start a story is at the beginning . . . of every·thing that happens in the story.

If you're writing fiction, the best place to start a story is right in the middle of the action . . . on the day that something is different.

So start with things happening. Show your character doing something or talking to someone.

An excellent beginning is to show the character doing something that reveals what he is good at or what he fears. (You'll use those traits later in the story when the character faces the final obstacle and uses some·thing he's good at to overcome it. See "Tell a Story," page 97.)

After you get the story going, you can then fill in more about the set·ting and give readers the background they need to understand what's going on. Remember, show only *significant* details when you describe a setting. Choose details to reveal the character's mood, or details that are important to the plot.

For example, there's an old saying that if you show a shotgun over the fireplace in chapter one, the gun must go off by the last chapter!

If, toward the end of the story, your character needs a rope to tie a boat to a pier because he'll need the boat to make his escape, show readers the rope early in the story. You don't have to make a big deal out of it. Just mention it in passing: *an old rope lay coiled in the corner of the boathouse.* Later, when the character needs a rope, readers will remember, *Oh, yeah! There's a rope in the boathouse!*

That way, readers feel like they're part of the story – and they feel smart that they figured it out.

> "The last thing that we find in making a book is to know what we must put first."
>
> Blaise Pascal (1623–1662), French philosopher, mathematician, physicist, and author

If you're writing nonfiction, such as a magazine article or report for school, you still want to make your beginning interesting. Your beginning – also known as the *opening lead* – can be one sentence, a paragraph, or several paragraphs (as long as you quickly get to the point).

An opening lead has three jobs:

1. Get your readers' attention and interest!

Something in the details, the situation, or your tone (some humor, a small mystery noticed, a question raised) should be intriguing.

2. Introduce the topic.

First, you must be clear in your own mind. Answer the question, "What is this story about?"

Be sure to narrow the focus to just one aspect of the subject. An article about "dogs," for example, is too general. The reader will want to know, "What about dogs?" Instead, make the topic something like choosing a puppy, or the care and feeding of your dog, or kind of jobs dogs do for people.

3. Set the tone of the article.

If your writing is funny, your lead should be funny. If it's a happy story, use shorter sentences with strong verbs for more energy. If it's a sad story, write longer sentences to make the reader read slowly.

✔ Writing Tip

If you're having trouble deciding how to start an article or story, start writing the middle part first.

Once you get going, an idea for a great lead may come to you. Even if it doesn't, you'll be well on your way to a finished piece of writing . . . instead of wasting an hour staring at a blank piece of paper or computer screen.

MARY-LANE KAMBERG

Types of Opening Leads

Different kinds of leads work best for different topics and different audiences. Many writers try out two or three different leads for a story until they find the one that "feels" right.

Here are some ways to get your reader interested in reading on. You may notice similarities among the different types. That's because they often overlap.

In fact, you can try combinations of two or more types if it suits what you're writing. Pulling the reader into the story is what's most important, not worrying about the correct label for the type of lead.

Although these "grand openings" here are for nonfiction writing, you can also use them to start short stories, poems, and other types of writing.

"Bring all your intelligence to bear on your beginning."

Elizabeth Dorothea Cole Bowen (1899–1973), Anglo-Irish novelist and short-story writer

Make a startling statement.
Short and quick, this lead contains an element of surprise that makes the reader curious. It also leads right into the subject of the story or report.

```
City traffic engineers want to blow up a bridge.
   That's why they're requesting money to redesign
the roadway at the intersection of 13th St. and Ash.
```

Write a twist on something familiar.
Take a familiar saying . . . and change it in some way to add humor or simply get attention.

```
There's no place like home.
   For a school.
```

Tell a story.

Readers love stories, so start your piece with one.

"Story" doesn't mean something that isn't true, but something that has a character, and a little drama, to create a situation that an individual reader could relate to.

> Jennifer never liked her nose. It was too wide and too long with a hump and a downward hook. Still, the 16-year-old high school student never dwelled on it until a classmate teased her with a hand-drawn picture.
>
> After that, when people looked at her, she was sure they were thinking, *Look at that nose!*

Speak directly to the reader.

Bring your readers into your story by placing them smack in the middle of the topic.

> Your eyes itch. Your throat burns. Your nose is stuffy. Or runny. You have a cold. Or an allergy.
>
> You need help!
>
> Before you take any medicine, here's what you should know.

Ask questions.

Ask a series of questions that need no answer but illustrate the types of issues the article will talk about.

> What's the best brand of tennis racket? Which foods do athletes need? When should you start a preseason training program?
>
> And most important, where do you turn for advice?

MARY-LANE KAMBERG

Compare the past, present, or future.

> Tammy Kincaid was always good at math. And in eighth grade, she decided to pursue a career in accounting. Today she manages the city's leading accounting firm, and her job involves a lot more than numbers.

Here's another past, present, or future comparison lead that also includes a startling statement:

> Last October, Julie tried cocaine for the first time.
>   By August she was hospitalized for addiction.

Quote someone.

Start your story with conversation. Use something someone said to draw the reader in. (For nonfiction, quote a person you interviewed or a famous person's speech or book. In fiction, start with dialogue.)

> "The car salesman took me for a ride – literally," said Jeremy Brown, who bought his first car the day he turned 18. "I bought more car than I needed for too much money. I'll never let that happen again."

Make a list.

List a series of items or phrases that give readers a hint of your topic. Be sure to end the list with a simple statement or question that tells readers the point of the story.

> Pens, notebooks, calculators, rulers, markers, dividers, erasers, graph paper. And a book bag to carry them in.
>   Who knew school supplies could be hazardous to your health?

Compare two unlike things.

Use comparisons to help readers understand what you're talking about. Similes (something is *like* something else) and metaphors (something *is* something else) are usually thought of as poetry techniques, but they're also used in fiction and nonfiction.

Here's a comparison lead for a magazine article about a mall security guard.

> Like Air Force planes flying cover over the White House, Bert Hanson patrols the Lone Elm Mall.
>
> In fact, Hanson is a retired Air Force pilot, who now spends his days protecting shoppers, arresting shoplifters, and helping lost children find their mothers.

▶ *Definition: Metaphor*
A metaphor is a comparison of two unlike things that says one *is* the other.

▶ *Definition: Simile*
A simile is a comparison of two unlike things, linked by *like* or *as.*

Use statistics, numbers, and facts.

Readers often find surprising numbers, measurements, or fun facts are a good reason to read on.

> Results of a recently released five-year survey of college graduates shows that 59.6 percent no longer work for the first company that hired them. Of those, 74.2 percent left within the first two years on the job.
>
> Is lack of job satisfaction widespread?

(The following examples, which define a problem or paint a picture, also include statistics and numbers to interest the reader.)

Present a problem.

Stating a problem at the beginning of a story tells readers that a solution will soon follow. If they're interested in the problem, they'll want to read on to see how it was solved.

This example is reprinted from *Hydro Review Magazine* with permission:

> Fewer than 50 years after James W. Marshall discovered gold at Sutter's Mill and a mere 24 years after the transcontinental railroad linked California with the eastern United States, California's population had grown to 250,000. What began as the Gold Rush migration continued as the railroad brought more people into the state and provided the means to send goods back east to market.
>
> The state's citrus crop had blossomed. All the growers needed was a way to get oranges – their No. 1 cash crop – from their groves to Eastern grocery stores without spoiling and at a competitive price.
>
> For that, they needed ice – big blocks of it.

Paint a picture.

Describe someone, something, or some place by painting a "word picture" that readers can see for themselves.

> At birth, Amy's footprint was the size of her mother's thumbprint. Fourteen weeks premature, she weighed in at 1 pound, 14 ounces and measured 13 inches long. She could wear her mother's wedding ring on her thigh.

Whichever type of lead you choose, immediately follow it with a clear, brief sentence that tells readers what the article is about.

Then move on to the middle (see next chapter).

⇨ **Try this!**

Gather six issues of your favorite magazine together and read the beginning of each article. See if you can identify the type of opening lead the writer used.

Start a collection of article openings you like – ones that grab you right from the first sentences and make you want to read the article. Make a note of which techniques the author used.

⇨ **Try this!**

The next time you have to do a report for school, write three different types of beginnings. Then, pick the one that works best.

⇨ **Try this!**

Read the openings of five novels. Do any of them use a type of opening lead like the ones described in this chapter?

⇨ **Try this!**

Read a magazine article.

Now, write a different type of beginning for it!

⇨ **Try this!**

Pick a story or essay you have already written. Write two different beginnings, using the examples in this chapter.

Which works best?

Organize the Muddle in the Middle

Once your beginning has grabbed your readers' attention and interest, your task is to decide the order to tell readers what you know.

For most articles or stories, the middle part will have the major portion of what the piece is about.

But what order will you use to share your information with readers?

If you're writing a novel, a short story, or a nonfiction story full of drama, you might use the narrative form (see "Tell a Story," page 97) for your middle. This follows a main character (real or fictional) through the story . . . .setting out to get something he or she wants to achieve, encountering obstacles, and near the end, facing a dark moment . . . before reaching a goal.

If you're writing an article or report, you want to present a series of main points and helpful examples.

The topic and type of writing you're doing often dictate the way you organize the middle.

Here are four effective ways to present information:

"The whole is that which has beginning, middle, and end."

Aristotle (384–322 B.C.), Greek philosopher. His work *Poetics* **defined the structure and types of poetry.**

Chronological order

You seldom want to start a story at the "true" beginning, but instead with something most interesting (like a question, a quote, a picture, and all the other opening techniques).

So, after you've opened with an attention-grabbing lead, you can go back to the true beginning and tell the story in the order it happened. This order works well for short stories and novels, and also when you're writing a real-life story.

Step-by-step

If you are writing a how-to (see "How To Write a How-To," page 75), simply start with Step 1 and follow it with Steps 2, 3, 4, and so on.

Easy to difficult

When you are writing something full of scientific, technical, or other special information that might be hard for someone new to the subject to grasp, arrange your main points and examples from the easiest to understand to the most difficult.

That way, the information that readers get early in the article or report will help them understand the more complex ideas toward the end.

Anticipate reader's questions

This order works well when you are writing news stories, but you can use it in reports or other articles, too.

The trick: once you cover the basic 5 Ws and the H (see "Report the News," page 63) to open the story, and you clearly state the point of the story, ask yourself, "What would my readers want to know next?"

Once you have a list of a few questions that many readers would have, answer those questions . . . in the order you think the readers would be likely to ask them.

⇨ **Try this!**

Choose three different magazines that publish nonfiction articles.

Read several articles in each magazine. Can you identify the order the writer chose to present the information?

If you find a way to present information not listed above, write it in here:

_____

_____

Expert Exits

Do you hate good-byes?

Leaving friends or relatives at the end of a visit can be hard. Sometimes it's also hard to say good-bye to your reader at the end of a story or article.

So . . . end your piece of writing in a way that satisfies readers and lets them feel a sense that the story or poem is complete.

Just as writers use a wide variety of opening leads, they also use a wide variety of endings. Here are some of them.

(You might notice that many types of opening leads also work well as endings.)

"All's well that ends well."

William Shakespeare (1564–1616), English poet and one of the world's best-known playwrights

Summary statement

Restate the main points of the story. It may be a simple statement or a list of the points covered.

```
With preseason screening, safe training techniques,
and protective gear, you'll decrease your chance of
a sports injury.
```

Call to action

Encourage readers to *do* something. This is an important type of ending for advertising. It also works well for persuasive speeches or letters to the editor.

```
So, see your dentist twice a year. You'll have
cleaner teeth. And, regular appointments help find
cavities early when they're easy to fix.
```

Quote

Let the people that you write about also end the story for you.

```
Barry Nelson loves his new house. "It's bright,
colorful, and cheerful," he says.
  "And the best part is: it's new."
```

What's next?

To end an article about something that has been accomplished, look ahead. What's next?

Use the answer as your ending.

```
Future activities will include learning what worked
in the past, checking the cost of planned improve-
ments, and working to gain community support.
```

✔ Writing Tip

Once you write the end of your story, re-read the entire story … without making corrections. See if it flows from sentence to sentence.
If something seems not quite right, but you can't tell what it is, try turning the story "upside-down." Use the ending for the beginning and write "backwards" to the middle. (Note: You'll need a new ending!)

Question

If you've presented both sides of a controversy, and final decisions are yet to be made, end with questions that keep readers thinking about the subject of your article.

```
So, will the city council vote to ban smoking in
restaurants? And if they do, will restaurant owners
close their doors?
```

Talk to the reader

Speaking directly to the reader is a good way to say, "Good·bye."

> You'll have to solve your own problems. But with advice from experts, you're better prepared to fix what's wrong.

Finish the story

If you start the article with a brief story, come back to it at the end. Remember the "Paint a picture" lead (see page 39) about the baby?

> At birth, Amy's footprint was the size of her mother's thumbprint. Fourteen weeks premature, she weighed in at 1 pound, 14 ounces and measured 13 inches long. She could wear her mother's wedding ring on her thigh.

To finish the article, finish the story:

> Today Amy is a first grader at Meadow Lane Elementary School. She wears glasses and lags behind other kids her age in reading skills. But she's doing better than her parents thought she would.
>   "She's our miracle baby," her mother says.

Full circle

Go back to the beginning. This ending is similar to the "Finish the story" ending, except there is no "story." You just take readers back to the beginning and show that something has changed.
  If your beginning was:

> White sand beaches and breathtaking sunsets off Florida's Gulf Coast welcome visitors to Sarasota.

Your full-circle ending can be:

It's sunrise in Sarasota. Time to leave.
   With memories to last a lifetime.

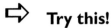 **Try this!**

Look at a story you have already written.
   Write two different endings, using suggestions from this list.

Section II

Write, Write, Write

9 Steps for Great Writing

When professional writers write, they often use nine steps to get their work ready to publish.

These steps may happen quickly.

Or they may happen over the course of a few weeks . . . or even longer.

But a good author knows about these steps to great writing, and knows where in the process they are with each piece.

Here's how the writing process works, from beginning idea to sharing your finished work with others:

"I have always been in a condition in which I cannot not write."

Barbara Tuchman (1912–1989), American historical writer and winner of two Pulitzer Prizes

Step 1. Idea

Before you write, you need an idea. For nonfiction (writing about real people, things, or events), it helps to narrow your topic enough that you don't have to include every fact there is about it.

For instance, instead of writing about "trees" in general, write about trees native to your state, shade trees, fruit trees, planting trees . . . or the fun of climbing a tree.

For fiction, start with a character who faces a problem. (See "Tell a Story," page 97.)

Step 2. Information

The next step is gathering information, also called research. Research means looking for information from other people, books, or the Internet. It also means using your own observations.

▶ *Definition: Research*

Research is looking for information from other people, books, or the Internet or using your own observations.

Step 3. First draft

Start writing! Write fast. For fiction, start with your character doing something. For nonfiction, write from memory. You will remember the facts that most interested you. Write them down.

If you leave something out, you can add it later. If you include too much, you can remove it later.

For now, get words on paper. (See also "Free Writing," page 28.)

Step 4. Time off

Once you have a first draft of your story, poem, or report, shove it in a drawer. Take time away from it. If you can, wait several days before reading it.

If you need to turn it in the next day, at least set it aside and work on homework in a different subject for a while. Rest your brain.

Step 5. Editing

Later, go back and read your work. Look for places you can improve it by adding or taking away information, adding dialogue or quotes, and finding a better word for one you used.

If you notice spelling or punctuation errors, change them (but you will look harder for these in Step 8).

Read the work aloud. Make changes where you stumble over words or phrases.

Step 6. Peer review

You might not want anyone to see your first draft – or even your second, third, or fourth! But, at some point, showing your work to a friend who also likes to write can help you improve it.

Ask what he or she likes best and which parts seem boring or confusing. Ask for suggestions to make your writing better. Listen to your friend's ideas. (See "Critique Checklist," page 106.)

However, this is *your* writing. If you disagree about one or more ideas, take a few minutes to think it over. Try to look at your work the way someone else sees it. If you still disagree, leave it the way you had it.

Step 7. Rewrite

Rewrite your piece of work, including whatever changes you think can make the writing stronger.

Step 8. Proofread

This is the step where you make your work as good as it can be. Check spelling, grammar, and punctuation.

Look for better ways to say what you want to say: different word choices, fewer words, and adding or deleting facts or characters.

Step 9. Share your work

When you're finished, you're ready to share your work with readers. If you're working on a school assignment, your teacher is your reader. If you are writing stories or poems for fun, share them with friends.

Look for places to publish your work: perhaps a school newspaper, a literary magazine, a contest for young writers, or online.

(See "Where To Submit Your Work for Publication," page 121.)

⇨ Try this!

Write a short story or report just for fun following all 9 steps of the writing process. At the end, compare your first draft and your final copy. Did the changes you made improve the work?

Practice Makes Professional

If you shoot 25 free-throws every day, you'll become a better free-throw shooter. If you draw a picture every day, you'll become a better artist. If you play the same song on a piano every day, you'll become a better musician.

The same goes for writing.

Everything you write makes you a better writer. That's because writing is problem solving. Writers have to make decisions in every sentence.

Which word should I use?

What shall I name my character?

Shall I tell about the new shoes before I tell about the dance recital?

The more times you solve problems in your writing, the more ready you'll be to solve similar writing problems in the future.

✔ Writing Tip

Professional writers know that their work improves if they write every day. You don't have to turn out a chapter of a novel, or even a complete poem.

But if you write for ten or fifteen minutes every day without worrying about spelling or grammar or even whether what you say makes sense, you'll become a better writer.

When you practice writing, you are free to write about whatever you want. And while you're writing, if something comes to you that is off the subject, go with it! It doesn't matter. Just keep putting words on paper.

Write a poem.

Or start a story about a character you make up.

Write about something that really happened.

Write real and imagined conversations.

Write a letter to an imaginary friend.

Describe a fight you had – or would like to have – with a real person.

MARY-LANE KAMBERG

(Write the words you'd like to speak. Imagine – and write – what the other person might say.)

An easy way to practice writing is to "free write." (See "Writing Tip," page 28.) At the end of 10 or 15 minutes, you might have the beginning of a really great story or poem.

Or, you might have nonsense.

It doesn't matter. You practiced writing.

The next time you write something, you'll already be a better writer.

> "Writing everyday is a way of keeping the engine running, and then something good may come out of it."
>
> T.S. Eliot (1888–1965), poet best known for *The Wasteland* and winner of the Nobel Prize in Literature

✔ Writing Tip

Football players and other athletes warm up their muscles before they practice or play a game.

If you have a writing assignment for school, free-writing is a good way to warm up your brain. If you have an essay or report to write, start your homework session with 10 minutes of free-writing . . . about anything.

By free-writing you help your brain adjust to "writing mode." After warming up, take a look at the writing assignment.

Do another free-writing session, but this time write about the assigned material. When the timer sounds, you already have some ideas you can use for your assignment.

Chalise Bourque Miner, author of *Rainforest Girl,* says, "Writing every day is like hopping on your bike and riding the neighborhood. You could ride for days and never see an interesting bird or squirrel.

"But there may be the day you discover the greatest garage sale with the entire Harry Potter set, or a ring with your birthstone, or baby kittens and your mom lets you keep one.

"Writing is that way. Lots of times all you get is the ride. But you have to be out there to see that one great sunset that becomes your best summer poem."

 Try this!

Make an appointment with yourself to write for 10 minutes at a certain time of day every day for a week.

Open a book or newspaper, or grab a cereal box.

Write down any sentence from it.

Set a timer for 10 minutes.

Now, write a story using the sentence as the beginning.

Write fast. Keep your pencil moving until the timer rings.

"It is by sitting down
to write every morning
that one becomes a writer."

Gerald Brenan (1894–1987),
English historian

Dear Diary

Write about your life experiences. Write about your dreams. Write about your questions.

A good place for this kind of writing is in a diary, or journal. A journal is a personal record of your experiences and observations. It's usually kept in either an ordinary notebook or a special book made for that purpose.

> "A good writer needs only one good reader, even if that reader be the writer himself."
>
> Henry Miller (1891–1980), American novelist

Some writers use a loose-leaf notebook with subject dividers so they can put all their writing about the same topic together.

Whatever form a journal takes, it's about *you* – your truest thoughts and feelings. And it's meant for only you to read. Keep it in a safe place – maybe even a place that locks – so you feel comfortable putting down your secrets.

A journal is a place to practice writing without worrying about spelling, grammar, or punctuation. It's a place to be yourself, a place to get to know yourself. Writing in a journal is a different kind of practice writing: it's a conversation with yourself.

✔ Writing Tip

You can use a journal to experiment with different kinds of writing. Try a poem. Or, if you're trying to make a decision, write about it in your journal. Tell your journal both sides of the issue. Argue in favor of both decisions.

Or try to persuade yourself to change your mind about something.

Record your observations of the day. Record what you experienced through your senses of sight, sound, smell, taste, and touch. What did the experiences remind you of?

Or just have fun. Write silly rhymes. Invent strange new words and ridiculous stories that could never happen – or could they?

Many writers write in a journal every day. They record things they noticed that day. They comment on their observations.

For example, one writer wrote about feeding pieces of bread to the birds at the park. She noticed that one bird always tried to grab two or three pieces, while the other birds took only one at a time. She asked her journal whether the bird was greedy or just very hungry. She compared the bird to humans that she knew.

She asked herself, *if I were a bird, would take only one piece of bread at a time or would I grab all I could get?*

✔ **Writing Tip**

If you can't think of anything to write about in your journal, turn back to an earlier page and read something you wrote. Have you changed your mind about what you said that day? Write about something else related to the subject.

Sometimes writers use ideas from their journals to write stories, essays, or poems. Sometimes they just let the journal be . . . a journal. The only rules for writing in your journal are rules you make up. And if you make up rules, you can always change them.

Your journal is yours. You only have to please yourself.

⇨ **Try this!**

Write in a journal or diary every day for a month. At the end of the month, ask yourself if writing in a journal is a habit you would like to continue. If so, keep it up!

⇨ **Try this!**

Write something that happened that made you happy, sad, frightened, or safe. Record any physical feelings you experienced (stomach ache, the touch of a soft blanket, etc.) Why did you react this way?

MARY-LANE KAMBERG

Sound Off

What's in the news? What do you think about it?

What should we do about global warming? Which candidate do you support for governor? What should city government do about the condition of the sidewalks in the old part of town? Did an article in the newspaper make you angry? Why?

Make your thoughts count. Write them in a short essay.

Use it as a letter to the editor of the "opinion and editorial" section of your local newspaper. (The name of this section often is shortened to Op-Ed.)

"Every author really wants to have letters printed in the papers. Unable to make the grade, he drops down a rung of the ladder and writes novels."

P. G. Wodehouse (1881–1975), British-born novelist and screenwriter

Before you start, read letters the newspaper has published in the past. That will give you an idea of the kinds of letters the editor likes.

Some editors get few letters, and publish almost every one they receive. Other editors – especially those in large cities – get more letters than they have space to publish. In that case, your letter must compete with those sent by other readers.

Here are some tips for letters to the editor that have a good chance of publication:

Keep it short.

Newspaper space is limited, so a short letter has a better chance of being published than a long one.

Write a brief title for your letter.

Give your letter a title that tells the editor your subject at a glance: "Recycle Plastic," "Broken Sidewalks," or "Jones for Governor."

This type of title is called a "keyword slugline" in the news business.

▶ Definition: keyword slugline

In the news industry, a keyword slugline states the subject of a story or letter to the editor. According to the Associated Press, a keyword slugline should have no more than 21 letters.

Choose a topic that's in the news.

People want to read about what's "new," so choose a subject people are talking about. If you want to write about something that has been debated for a long time, tie your letter to a current news story . . . or present a new way to look at the old issue.

Start with a sentence that explains the topic and why it's important.

In addition to telling the editor your subject, let the editor – and later your readers – know what your letter is about.

If you're responding to something you read in an earlier edition of the newspaper, start your letter with something like, "In the *Daily News* article about the condition of city sidewalks (April 23), your reporter failed to mention the danger of falls by older citizens caused by tripping on the broken concrete."

Clearly state your opinion.

Say: "The city needs to repair the sidewalks." You might speak about why your opinion is important to everyone. "Now that the weather is nice, more people take walks." Or, you can personalize the issue. "My grandfather tripped and broke his leg because . . ."

Stick to one viewpoint.

In news stories, reporters describe both sides of an issue. But in an opinion essay, feel free to stick only to your own opinion. Or, state a point on the other side of the issue, but argue your side.

> The opposition will say new sidewalks cost too much, but can we afford to let our neighborhoods crumble?

State accurate facts and statistics.

Check reliable sources on the Internet or ask your librarian for help. If you state a fact, also state where you got the information.

> The U.S. Census Bureau says the percentage of U.S. citizens older than age 50 is growing.

End with a call to action.

What should be done? What's your remedy? Tell readers what you want them to do.

> Urge the city council to authorize money for repairs.

Sign your first and last name and include your contact information.

Newspapers won't publish anonymous letters. Also, before most editors print letters from the public, they like to contact those who wrote them to verify that they're the ones who wrote and sent the letters.

   Make it easy for them. Include your address, telephone number, and e-mail address (yours or a parent's). Also, it's a good idea to say "contact information is not for publication." Like this:

> Contact information (not for publication):
> 1234 Main St.
> City, State ZIP
> (123) 456-7890
> youngwriter@internetserver.com

   Also include your grade and name of the school if you want to. (It might make the editor choose your letter instead of someone else's because so few young people write to them.)

Proofread for grammar, spelling, and punctuation.

Editors will make minor changes, if necessary. But if your letter has too many mistakes, the editor won't take the time to fix them. Your letter won't be published.

Use humor, if appropriate.

Your letter has a good chance of getting published, if you use humor for appropriate topics. In this case, ignore the "rules" above. Just keep your letter short and sweet (and funny!).

For example, in the *Olathe Daily News* (a newspaper for a Kansas town on the Santa Fe Trail), the Chamber of Commerce asked for suggestions for slogans to encourage tourists to visit. The town had few attractions . . . but it was home to the county jail. The editor published the letter from one reader who wrote:

> Here's my suggestion for the tourism slogan:
>   "Go directly to jail on the Santa Fe Trail."

Mail or e-mail your letter.

Send your letter to the "Letters to the Editor" department (or whatever is the specific name of that section of your newspaper).

For example, in some newspapers, the section might be called "News and Views" or some other catchy title. (The address likely is listed on the editorial page of the newspaper. If not, call the business office and ask for the correct address.)

Watch for your letter in print.

Read every issue of the newspaper for a week or two to see if your letter appears.

 Try this!

Think of a current topic that you have strong feelings about.

Write an essay and mail it to the editor of your school newspaper or community newspaper.

Sell the Sizzle!

Advertising is a specialized field of writing aimed at selling products, services, political candidates, and ideas. An advertising copywriter is the person who writes the words in newspaper, magazine, and online ads, as well as the scripts for radio and television commercials. The words are called copy.

> "Don't sell the steak – sell the sizzle."
>
> Elmer Wheeler (1905–1968), known as "American's No. 1 Salesman," published 20 books.

▶ *Definition: Copy*

The "copy" (used as a noun) is the text (the written words) of an advertisement, news story, or magazine article.

▶ *Definition: Copyright*

Legal protection for authors that prohibits others from copying their work without permission. Copyright applies to books, poems, newspaper and magazine articles, songs, movie scripts, photographs, and other creative work. When an author allows someone to publish his or her work, it really means allowing the "right to make copies."

The goal of advertising writing is to sell. A well-known slogan in the advertising business is "Don't sell the steak, sell the sizzle." That means you want to appeal to customers on an emotional level, rather than a logical one.

Tempt them with the enjoyment and pleasure they will get from seeing the steak, smelling it cook, hearing the sizzle on the grill, tasting the steak, "touching" the texture of the steak. In other words, help customers imagine the senses they will experience from the steak.

To write a good ad, the copywriter must first get a customer's attention and interest him or her in the product or service. The goal is to make the customer want the product and become convinced that he or she "must" have it. The final step is to get the customer to take action:

buy the product or service, vote for the candidate, or change his or her mind to accept a new idea.

To motivate a customer takes more than one ad or commercial. So an important part of advertising is repetition. The more times customers see or hear the same message, the more likely they are to act.

The key to successful advertising is to answer the customer's question, "What's in it for me?" The way to answer that question is to show the benefits of what you're trying to sell.

Here's how to write advertising copy:

Step 1. Make a list of the features of what you're trying to sell.

What is the size, weight, color, brand name, fabric, etc.? If you want to sell a steak, for instance, the list of features would include such items as:

- ▶ Type of steak: T-bone
- ▶ Weight of steak: 6-ounces
- ▶ How it is cooked: charcoal-grilled to order
- ▶ What spices are used: garlic and other spices
- ▶ Nutritional content:
  - ✔ 336 calories
  - ✔ 40 percent fat
  - ✔ 46.2 grams of protein
  - ✔ Zero carbohydrates (no sugar)
  - ✔ 120 milligrams of sodium (low sodium)
  - ✔ High in iron, niacin, phosphorous, vitamin B12, and zinc

These facts sound boring. Would you run right out to buy a T-bone if you read an ad that sounded like this?:

Buy a 6-ounce T-bone steak for dinner, charcoal-grilled to your order with garlic and other spices. A T-bone steak has 336 calories. It's 40 percent fat and has 46.2 grams of protein, zero carbohydrates,

MARY-LANE KAMBERG

and 120 milligrams of sodium. It's also high in iron, niacin, phosphorous, vitamin B12, and zinc.

Step 2. Beside each feature, write a benefit to the buyer.

Listing features of a product appeals to the customer's brain, not the emotions. You'll be more successful with advertising if you use product benefits to appeal to a customer's emotions through the five senses.

Your job as an advertising copywriter is to communicate the benefits of these features.

What can you say about the feature that is good for the customer?

- ▶ Type: T-bone = "a traditional favorite of steak lovers!"
- ▶ Weight: 6-ounces = "a nice size for a main course"
- ▶ How it's cooked: charcoal-grilled to order = "cooked the way you like it"
- ▶ What spices are used: garlic and other spices = "garlic tastes good"
- ▶ Nutritional content:
  - ✔ 336 calories = "furnishes 17 percent of daily calories needed for a 2,000-calorie diet"
  - ✔ 40 percent fat = "makes the steak juicy"
  - ✔ 46.2 grams of protein = "a good source of protein"
  - ✔ Zero carbohydrates (no sugar) = "good for low-carb diets"
  - ✔ 120 milligrams of sodium (low sodium) = "reduces health risks"
  - ✔ High in iron, niacin, phosphorous, vitamin B12, and zinc = "provides good nutrition"

Step 3. Start the ad with something to get the customer's attention and interest.

Use the senses to show the benefits you want to feature. Ask for the sale with a phrase like "buy it today!" Give information about where the customer can buy the product.

Does the following ad do a better job than the first one?

```
What's for dinner? How about a juicy, 6-ounce T-
bone steak? You'll love the aroma of steak sizzling
on the grill. Taste the tender beef flavored with
garlic and fresh-ground pepper, cooked just the way
you like it. We have your table waiting!
Sam's Steak House, 1234 S. Main St.
```

⇨ **Try this!**

Think of something you own. Pretend that you want to sell it.

First, list its features and benefits.

Then, write an ad.

⇨ **Try this!**

Read the copy in an ad you find in a magazine or newspaper (or listen carefully to a commercial on radio or television).

Listen for features and benefits.

Did the copywriter use all the senses to sell you the product, the service, or the idea?

Report the News

If you like to know what's happening, you may have a "nose for news." If you can "sniff out" an interesting story, you might like being a reporter for a newspaper or radio or television station.

Writing a news story is different from writing an essay, short story, or novel. Those kinds of writing need a beginning, a middle, and an end. But news stories often use a different order, known as the *inverted pyramid.*

Think of the shape of a news story as an upside-down triangle.

> "When a dog bites a man, that is not news, because it happens so often. But if a man bites a dog, that is news."
>
> John B. Bogart (1845–1921), editor of the *New York Sun* newspaper

This style of writing began during the American Civil War. Reporters who witnessed and wrote about the battles often sent their stories back to their newspaper offices using the telegraph.

Unfortunately, the telegraph lines often went down – sometimes accidentally and sometimes on purpose as a way to keep enemy commanders from talking to each other. If a reporter told his story in the order it happened, the piece wouldn't give the winner of the battle until the end of the story.

But if the telegraph line went down while the reporter was sending the story, the story was interrupted . . . and the newspaper editor in a faraway town wouldn't know who won the battle.

That's why reporters started putting the most important and most interesting information in the first paragraph of the story. They made sure to answer six questions at the beginning: who, what, when, where, why, and how. (These questions are now known as the 5 Ws and the H.)

That way, if the telegraph lines went down in the middle of sending the story, newspaper readers would still get the most important news of the day.

▶ *Definition: Inverted pyramid*
A story order, used in news reporting, where a summary appears in the first paragraph, followed by information decreasing in interest or importance.

▶ *Definition: "The 5 Ws and the H"*
Answers to who, what, when, where, why, and how, that appear in the first paragraph of a news story.

The first paragraph of a news story is called the opening lead – often just called "the lead."

After first answering the 5 Ws and the H, reporters ranked the information they had left over. After the first paragraph, they asked themselves, "If I can tell the reader only one more thing before the telegraph line goes down, what would it be?" One way to help decide was to ask, "What would the reader want to know next?"

Reporters kept asking themselves the same question over and over, until they told everything they knew. When they finished, the most important and most interesting information lay early in the story. The least important and least interesting information fell at the end.

▶ *Definition: Opening lead*
The beginning of a news or feature story.

▶ *Definition: Feature story*
A human-interest article in a newspaper or magazine.

The inverted pyramid is an upside-down triangle that the news would look like if the most important information were written in the biggest letters, like this:

The very most important fact
The next most important fact
The next most important fact
The next most important fact
The next most important fact
The next most important fact
The next most important fact
The next most important fact
The next most important fact
The next most important fact

Today, reporters still use the inverted pyramid. A benefit is that the editor can simply cut off the story at any point. The story loses only the least important information . . . if a bigger news story comes in at the last minute, or if an advertiser wants to place one more ad.

Here's an example of the first paragraph of a news story with the 5 Ws and the H identified.

```
[Who?] Two men . . . [What?] robbed the 1st National
Bank . . . [Where] at 12th and Main . . . [When]
yesterday at 12:30 p.m. . . . [How?] One man waited
outside in a 2008 black Ford pick-up truck, while
the other went into the bank and handed the teller
a note asking for money. . . . [Why?] When police
arrested the men, the driver said, "We needed the
money to buy our kids new shoes."
```

The reporter should now ask, "What will my readers want to know next?" They might want to know, "Was anyone hurt?"

If that's what the reporter decides, the next line would say, "The two tellers on duty were unharmed." And the line after that might be, "Because the robbery happened during the lunch hour, no customers were in the bank."

⇨ **Try this!**

Read a newspaper story that appears on the front page. Identify the 5 Ws and the H. Would you have made the same decisions about the order as the reporter who told the story?

Note: Not all stories in newspapers are news stories. Some are features, which are human-interest stories and usually follow narrative form. (See "Tell a Story," page 97.)

⇨ **Try this!**

Here are the facts of an imaginary news story. Write a paragraph with the 5 Ws and the H, plus one more sentence that reflects the next most important fact.

Decide the order to tell what happened. Finish the story yourself, adding other details in the order you think is important.

- ✔ It's been raining all week.
- ✔ The sheriff said, "Drivers should not drive into moving water."
- ✔ The Missouri River is 10 feet above flood stage.
- ✔ Three people died.
- ✔ The flood happened on Sunday afternoon.
- ✔ The dead were in their cars trying to cross moving water.
- ✔ The fire department rescue squad rescued an 8-year-old boy from a maple tree.
- ✔ He had climbed the tree to escape the flood.
- ✔ The flood happened in Kansas City, Missouri.

Write a Thank-You Note

All through your life, you receive gifts. Birthday gifts. Holiday gifts. Graduation gifts. When you get a present, acknowledge it with a thank-you note.

> "It's never too late to say, 'thank you.'"
>
> Ann Landers (1918–2002), advice columnist in American newspapers

You can e-mail your thank-you. But many givers – especially older ones – think e-mail is too casual. They prefer hand-written notes, as more personal.

Still, thanking the giver is what's most important. All you need to say is, "Thank you for [the book]." But a good thank-you note contains several additional elements (in any order):

> ▶ "Thank you" or some other words of appreciation. "I love my new . . ." or, "I'm grateful for your help for . . ."
>
> ▶ A specific mention of the item given. If you got a book, use the book's title instead of just "the book." If you got a sweater, say, "the red, wool sweater" instead of "the sweater." Be specific.
>
> ▶ A sentence about how much you like it, how you will use it, or why the gift is important to you. "I've wanted to read that book ever since it came out." Or, "Red is my favorite color."
>
> ▶ A sentence or two with a personal message for the giver. "It was nice to see you at my graduation party." Or, "You were nice to remember my birthday."
>
> ▶ A closing word like *love* or *sincerely*.
>
> ▶ Your name.

If you are thanking someone for sending money, leave out the specific amount. Instead, say something like, "the generous gift" or "the birthday money." For a cash gift, a mention of what you will do with the money is a nice touch: "I'm saving it toward a new bicycle." Or, "I'm excited to buy the new CD by [your favorite band]."

Here are two sample thank-you notes:

Dear Grandma and Grandpa,
Thank you so much for the book, How To Draw Horses. I'm getting pretty good at drawing other animals, but horses have been difficult for me. I will send you my first picture. I'm looking forward to seeing you at the farm in July.

Love,
(Your Name)

Dear Aunt Ginger,
I appreciate the money you sent to pay my first month's cell phone bill. I am so excited to have my own phone! Now I can stay in touch with my friends and keep up with everything that's going on. Thanks, too, for coming to my birthday dinner. I always love it when the whole family can be together.

Love,
(Your Name)

⇨ Try this!

Pretend you got a gift of $100 for middle-school graduation from your grandmother. Write a thank-you note.

⇨ Try this!

Aunt Amy got you a new computer game for your birthday. Write a thank-you note.

⇨ Try this!

Your best friend gave you a book that you really didn't like. Write a thank-you note without "lying" (saying you like it), but don't let her or him know you don't like the gift.

Remember

When a relative, friend, or pet dies, writing about the loss is a good way to deal with the grief. And helping others remember the one who died is one of the most important jobs a writer has.

> "No tears in the writer, no tears in the reader."
>
> **Robert Frost (1874–1963), popular American poet and winner of four Pulitzer Prizes**

Many people first experience such loss when a pet dies. "Saying good-bye to a pet is physical and affects the whole body," says Judith Bader Jones, poet and author of short-story collection *Delta Pearls.* "We miss the sight of our pet, but it is the loss of touch that we mourn . . . the physical feel of the fur and the heat from the body of a dog or a cat supports our desire to bond with life."

You might even experience a sense of grief when you misplace a favorite doll or break a favorite toy. Writing a memorial can help you deal with the loss.

One type of written memorial is an *obituary,* which is a published death notice. An obituary – sometimes called an *obit* for short – lets readers know that someone died. It often includes highlights of the person's life.

▶ *Definition: Obituary*
A death notice published in a newspaper, magazine, or online; usually includes a brief biography.

When you write a memorial, use specific words that a reader can picture, hear, taste, smell, and – especially – touch. That is the best way to help a reader feel the same sadness you feel.

On the next page, you'll find a "list poem" (see "Makin' a List Poem," page 83) written as a memorial. Writing this kind of poem is a good way to remember someone you love.

My Grandmother

dressed as Diamond Lil for Halloween
played solitaire
got her hair washed at the beauty parlor
planted petunias
canned wax beans from her garden
baked rhubarb pie
used tooth powder you pour in your hand
dried dishes with a flour sack
sewed doll clothes
recited poems she learned in school
sent money on my birthday

and once
before she died
said she loved me
  — Mary-Lane Kamberg

 Try this!

If you have experienced the death of a loved one or pet, write an essay or poem about the person or animal in a way that will help readers know the person or animal.

Use specific examples of things the loved one said or did.

 Try this!

Write a memorial essay or poem about a famous person in history.

 Try this!

Write a letter to a person or something that you miss.

Complain and Compliment

Has someone in a store gone the "extra mile" to help you? Has a restaurant server ignored you?

Either way, you might be so pleased (or so mad!) that you want to write a letter to the person's boss to compliment or complain about the service.

You could just jot down a short note that says "Miss Jones was awesome!" or "The waiter was rude!"

Here's an example of such a note:

Dear (store manager),
Last Tuesday I hurt myself in
front of your store. Miss Jones
helped me. She was awesome.

Sincerely,
(Your name)

However, like all good writing, the best letters use specifics to tell a story. Instead of telling the boss what the employee did, *show* the boss what happened.

A note that uses specific details a reader can picture is more effective:

Dear (store manager),
On Tuesday afternoon, I fell off my bicycle when the
chain broke in front of your store. I had no money and
no cell phone. My legs got pretty scraped up.
Miss Jones saw me through the window and ran out
to help me. She called my mom and helped me wash

"A compliment ought always precede a complaint, where one is possible, because it softens resentment and ensures for the complaint a courteous and gentle reception."

Mark Twain (1835–1910), American author of *The Adventures of Tom Sawyer* and *The Adventures of Huckleberry Finn*

"A compliment is verbal sunshine."

Robert Orben (1927–), American magician and comedy writer

off the dirt on my knee.

    I thought you'd like to know how one of your employees helped me. She's a really nice lady and cares about kids.

Sincerely,
(Your name)

Use of specific details also works if you write a letter of complaint. Suppose you were in line in a fast-food restaurant and the clerk ignored you and helped the adults behind you.

You might write something like this:

Dear (store manager),
I was at your restaurant on Saturday, and Steve was rude to me.

Sincerely,
(Your name)

What's the boss going to do with a note like that? Instead, use specific details. The boss will see what happened and why it was important.

In the following letter, the writer shows the boss that the clerk was rude without having to say the adjective *rude.* This letter of complaint suggests something the boss can do to keep the same thing from happening again.

When you complain to a manager of a store, it is a good idea to suggest a remedy.

Dear (store manager),
I was at your restaurant on Saturday and stood in "Steve's" line. I wanted to buy a cheeseburger and fries, and I had my own money. When it was my turn, Steve ignored me. He looked at the next person in line

and asked, "May I help you?"

That person was a mom with several kids, so I think Steve might have thought that I was with her. But, the next person in line was a teenager, just a few years older than I am. Again, Steve looked at the customer behind me and asked, "May I help you?"

I kept my money and rode my bike home. Tell your employees to treat all customers the same no matter how old they are.

Sincerely,
(Your name)

Finally, sign your name and give your contact information. No one pays attention to anonymous messages.

✔ Writing Tip

Your letter will have a bigger impact if you find the name of the person's boss and address the envelope directly to that person.

⇨ Try this!

Think of a time when someone in a store or restaurant was especially helpful or especially rude to you.

Write a letter of compliment or complaint to the manager.

There Ought To Be a Law!

Have you ever noticed something you thought was dangerous?

Do others do something that bugs you?

What would improve the world, the nation, or your hometown?

Senators, representatives, and state legislators work to create new laws. But sometimes ordinary citizens write and encourage passage of a new law. These individuals may not officially "be" writers, but they write, and their writing certainly is important.

> "Any fool can make a rule and every fool will mind it."
>
> Henry David Thoreau (1817–1862), American essayist and author of *Walden*

From time to time, city, state, and federal governments, as well as schools, businesses, sports associations, and other organizations have laws, rules, or policies that need change. Perhaps a law is unfair. Or the penalty is too hard . . . or too easy. Or, someone just thinks of a better way to do something.

Is the speed limit too fast? Too slow?

Should there be a 4-point shot in professional basketball?

Should everyone be required to take dancing lessons?

Should employees wear uniforms?

If you want to write a law, first think of what you want to accomplish. Then . . . start writing.

⇨ Try this!

1. Write a new law, rule, or policy for the real or imaginary world: a traffic law, a new policy for your school, a new rule for your favorite sport.

2. What should the penalty be for breaking the law or rule?

3. Ask your classmates if they think your idea would make a good law. See if they have a way to make the law you wrote better.

4. Explain why your law, rule, or policy is necessary.

MARY-LANE KAMBERG

How To Write a How-To

Can you serve a tennis ball? Pot a petunia? Strum a guitar?

You know how to do lots of things others would like to learn. If you write a how-to article, you can teach them!

A how-to article is like a recipe in a cookbook. In fact, a recipe is one form of a how-to. A recipe tells how to make cookies. A how-to article tells how to do other things.

Best of all, a how-to article is easy to write.

Here's how:

> "If you cannot teach me to fly, teach me to sing."
>
> Sir James Matthew Barrie (1860–1937), Scottish playwright and novelist; author of *Peter Pan*

Step 1. Write the beginning.

Answer the question: Why does your reader want to know how to do this? Add some encouragement with a phrase or sentence that says *You can do this!*

Use words like easy and simple. Or compare the activity to something else the reader is likely to be familiar with. Give the reader a reason to imagine the finished product or action with joy.

Step 2. List the supplies.

If some of the supplies are unusual or hard to find, give the reader a place to look for those special materials.

```
You'll find fabric glue in your favorite craft
store.
```

Step 3. List the steps.

The middle of the article is easy to write. Just list the steps in order. You can even say: Step 1, Step 2, Step 3. (Make a new paragraph for each step.)

Step 4. Say goodbye.

Write a simple ending. One good way is to show readers the benefit of knowing how to do what you just taught them.

Or tell them something like, "Now that you know how to do this task, you are ready to move on to a more difficult skill."

Or list some places they can go for more information.

Here's an example:

```
How To Wash Your Dog

If your dog needs a clean-up, here's how. It's like
washing your own hair!
    What you need: dog shampoo and conditioner, a
water tub, a hose, a sponge, and a towel.
    First, fill the tub with water with your hose.
Then, get your dog in the tub and put water all over
him or her.
    Second step: Next, get your sponge wet and put
shampoo on it. (Use however much you want.) Scrub
the sponge (in circles) around your dog until he/she
is poofy or bubbly.
    Third step: Rinse your dog completely. Then do
the same thing you did for the shampoo with the
conditioner.
    Final step: Rinse your dog and dry him/her.
    Now your dog is happy, and so are you! Also, you
now know how to wash your dog!
    - Audrey Phillips, 5th grade
```

⇨ **Try this!**

Write a how-to article about something you know how to do.

MARY-LANE KAMBERG

Recommend a Book

Have you read a book you enjoyed so much you want to tell others about it?

Write a book review.

A book review is like a book report, but writers write them for publication in newspapers, magazines, blogs, e·mails, and online publications.

When writing a review of a novel, follow these steps:

"There is more treasure in books than in all the pirate's loot on Treasure Island."

Walt Disney (1901–1966), American creator of Mickey Mouse and founder of Disneyland and Walt Disney World

Step 1.

Start with a strong opening paragraph. (See "Grand Openings," page 33.) Include the book title and the author's name in the first paragraph or so. (Some editors or readers also want the publisher's name, date of publication, retail price, or other information.)

Step 2.

Tell what the book is about in a single sentence. Fill in the blanks of narrative form (see "Tell a Story," page 97.) For instance: *[Book title] is about [name of character], who wants [what is the character's problem?].* For nonfiction, tell the main subject of the book.

Step 3.

For a novel, discuss some of the obstacles the character faces.

But let readers read the book themselves to learn the details of how the character confronts trouble. And keep them guessing about the ending.

For nonfiction, list the book's main points. Talk about which points particularly interested you.

Step 4.

Many readers like to know a little about a book's author and other books he or she has written, especially if the book is part of a series. Get this information from the book itself, or use a computer to Google the author's name for interesting facts to include in your review.

Step 5.

A book review also includes your opinions and reactions to the book. What did you like best? What did you like least?

Give your review balance. Some books are worth reading even if they have some slow spots or points that failed to interest you. Tell your reader about those issues, too.

Also, answer questions like:

▶ What made the character likeable?
▶ What is the villain like?
▶ What would you do differently if you wrote the book?
▶ What should the author have included but didn't?
▶ What was the best part? The worst?

Share your reviews with others who like to read. Send it in an e-mail to friends, or submit it for publication in a traditional or online magazine.

Here's an example of a book review:

Book Review
Magic Tree House #37: Dragon of the Red Dawn

Have you ever traveled through time and eaten sushi in good old Japan? You can almost taste the sushi when you read *Dragon of the Red Dawn* by Mary Pope Osborne. It feels just like you're there!

This book is number 37 in the Magic Tree House series written by Mary Pope Osborne. It is one of the nine Merlin missions available.

It is a Stepping Stone Book published by Random House Children's Books, a division of Random House, Inc., in New York City, New York. It was published in 2007 and illustrated by Sal Murdocca.

Dragon of the Red Dawn is about siblings Jack and Annie, who travel back in time to Edo (Tokyo), Japan, in the magic tree house to find a secret happiness for Merlin. Perhaps the happiness will make Merlin stop believing that he is dying.

Jack and Annie must get past the Samurai without a passport to get around the city of Edo. While they are there, a fire spreads throughout the city and they must help put it out.

After their friend's hut catches fire, they must save themselves. Then they must return to their tree house, again getting past the Samurai undetected to return to their own time.

Mary Pope Osborne is an award-winning author of many different books and series, such as a mystery series called Spider Kane and a Greek mythology series called Tales from the Odyssey, as well as the Magic Tree House series.

She has also written several books with her husband, Will Osborne, such as the Magic Tree House Research Guides and *Sleeping Bobby,* a retelling of a common fairy tale with a twist ending.

Dragon of the Red Dawn is one of my most favorite books of her Magic Tree House series.

My favorite part in the book is when Jack and Annie go to the tea house to get a bite to eat. They get sushi to eat, and have to eat with chopsticks. Annie learns how to use chopsticks faster than Jack. Jack almost gets them caught when a Samurai sees him struggling with his chopsticks.

My least favorite part in this book and each book of the series is when they start spinning in the tree house to go back in time. She uses the same exact wording in every book, and it gets tiring to read it over and over and over.

Besides that, I am ready to read every Magic Tree House book she writes, and she's still writing them.

One good thing about the books in the Magic Tree House Series is that each book stands alone.

I recommend that you read *Dragon of the Red Dawn* and all of the other Magic Tree House books if you dream of traveling through time and all over the world.

So check these books out at your local library, or buy them at a bookstore or a local discount store. A hardback copy costs only $11.95.

    – Thomas Fink, 5th grade

⇨ **Try this!**

Write a review of the last book you enjoyed.

⇨ **Try this!**

Write a review of a book you didn't like! Be specific about what things you did not like or found to be unsuccessful.

Be sure also to mention anything you *did* like.

Pack Your Poems with Punch

What does the sun looks like at dawn? What sounds do you hear on your way to school? Is your blanket soft or scratchy?

Do you know when your neighbor is grilling hamburgers outside? Can you tell if your toast is burnt?

How?

We experience the world by using the senses of sight, sound, touch, smell, and taste. Each of these senses offers ideas for writing. And the most important place to use them is in poetry

> "Good writing is supposed to evoke sensation in the reader – not the fact that it's raining, but the feeling of being rained upon."
>
> **E.L. Doctorow (1931–), American novelist, essayist, and short-story writer**

That's not to say you don't use sensory images in fiction and nonfiction. You do. In fact, using the senses makes all writing stronger. But in poetry, use of the senses is emphasized the most.

▶ *Definition: Concrete noun*
The name of a person, place, or thing that you can see, hear, taste, touch, or smell.

Nouns are good poem starters. The best ones are "concrete" nouns. That means nouns that you can experience using one or more of your five senses instead of just thinking about them or feeling the emotions.

Some examples of concrete nouns are *elephant, siren, thorn, butter,* and *firewood.* If you can see, hear, touch, taste or smell it, it's a concrete noun. Nouns that represent ideas – like *love, hate, happiness, sadness* – are less effective words in writing . . . because they mean different things to different readers. And readers understand them in their minds, not their emotions.

For example, *love* is a noun. It's the name of a thing. But you can't take a picture of love. It's a feeling. If you were going to draw a picture of love, what would you draw? A mother holding her baby? A child petting a puppy? Instead of telling your readers that the mother or the child loves the baby or puppy, *show* the reader what you *actually see,* and let the reader figure out that you are showing love.

As former Oklahoma poet laureate Betty Shipley (1931–1998) said, "If you give readers a choice between love and a kiss, they'll go for the kiss every time."

Using concrete nouns helps readers experience what you experience.

The next time you eat a candy bar or a fresh orange, pay attention to what is going on inside your mouth. As you go through your daily life, pay attention to what you see and hear, but also to what you touch, taste, and smell.

As you become more aware of your surroundings, you'll find lots of ideas for specific details to use when writing poems.

 Try this!

Look out the window. Write down five items that you see.

Then, close your eyes and put your fingertip on the paper.

Next, open your eyes and see which item your finger is closest to. Write a poem about it.

 Try this!

Close your eyes. Listen. Pay attention to each sound. Write down as many sounds as you hear.

Choose one and start a poem with that sound.

 Try this!

Collect five items from different rooms in your house. Hold each item for one minute.

Roll them around in your hand. Squeeze them.

Run your fingers over their surfaces.

Now, write a poem about one of them.

 Try this!

During the day, write down three things that you smell. Choose one smell and write a poem about what it brought to mind.

Makin' a List Poem

One of the easiest types of poems to write is the *list poem.* The list poem is, well, a list. The title ties the items on the list together.

Often, the last line adds some kind of twist or surprise.

Two main types of list poems are those that list nouns and those that list verbs.

List poems can rhyme, but they don't have to.

> *"Poetry is all nouns and verbs."*
>
> Marianne Moore (1887–1972), American poet who won both the National Book Award and the Pulitzer Prize

Write a list of nouns.

One way to write a noun list is to think of a place, action, or event. Then list nouns that pertain to the topic. Here's a list poem about a swimming pool:

Round Hill

a pool
a warm, dry towel
strong chlorine
a juicy hot dog
laughter
       – Becca Zeiger, 5th grade

✔ Writing Tip

Use the senses. When you're creating your list poem, include examples of sight, smell, sound, touch, and taste. In the above poem, the pool, towel, and hot dog provide the sense of sight. The chlorine and hot dog add the sense of smell. Laughter adds sound. The warm, dry towel adds the sense of touch. And the hot dog adds the sense of taste.

To write a list poem, think of a place you visited. Use its name as your title. Next, fill in the following list:

Name of the Place:
I saw . . .

_____

_____

I heard . . .

_____

_____

I touched . . .

_____

_____

I tasted . . .

_____

_____

I smelled . . .

_____

_____

After each phrase, fill in as many items as you can remember for each of the senses of sight, sound, touch, smell, and taste. (You can even make up some!) Here's an example:

Disneyland (my notes)
I saw . . . Mickey Mouse, fireworks, a parade
I heard . . . screams from the roller coaster, music
I touched . . . the rail of the roller coaster, my father holding my hand
I tasted . . . a cherry lollipop, popcorn
I smelled . . . popcorn popping

Select your favorite items from the list. Erase the rest. Arrange the remaining items in whatever order you like.

Erase the two starting words for each line.

Choose one of the items that adds something special or funny or sad and use it for the last line.

Disneyland

Mickey Mouse
screams from the roller coaster
fireworks
a cherry lollipop
my father holding my hand
        – Mary-Lane Kamberg

Write a verb list poem.

You can also use verbs for a list poem, which often uses a person's name as the title. The person becomes the subject of each line of the poem.

The title person can be an actual person you name, or a person identified by his or her job, such as a chef, a salesman, or a truck driver.

Here's an example of a list poem using verbs (and the poem also rhymes):

Lucia

Lucia

Jumps and
runs,
bounces,
sings;
cries and
yells,

dances,
swings.
Laughs and
skips,
hops and
giggles;
climbs and
falls,
twists and
wiggles.
Shouts and
screeches,
pushes,
shoves;
smiles,
kisses,
hugs and

loves.
        – Julia Marquez, 7th grade

✔ Writing Tip

In both poetry and prose, an extra line space tells the reader to pause. In the above poem, the pause is added to give more emphasis to the last line.

⇨ Try this!

Start with a place. Write a noun list poem.

⇨ Try this!

Start with a person or animal. Write a verb list poem.

Haiku for You

The use of concrete nouns is most important in *haiku* (pronounced "hi KOO"), a Japanese poetry form.

The goal of haiku is to recreate a moment in time when two images come together in an unusual, interesting, or surprising way.

Haiku usually has three lines: one short, one long, one short. In Japanese, the first line has five syllables, the second has seven, and the third has five.

However, Japanese differs from English. Japanese syllables are much shorter. So in modern haiku, poets who write in English often disregard the syllable count and simply write three lines, usually with the longest in the middle.

In fact, in modern haiku, some poets write only two lines – or just one!

Hundreds of haiku "rules" exist, but many contradict each other. Some generally agreed-upon characteristics include:

▶ Three lines without a title
▶ Little – or no – punctuation
▶ Lower-case letters (except for proper names)
▶ Seasonal reference
▶ Contrast
▶ Surprise

"A haiku is the expression of a temporary enlightenment, in which we see into the life of things."

Reginald H. Blyth (1898–1964), British haiku expert

✔ **Writing Tip**
Seasonal references in haiku can be a word or phrase. Some examples include *summer sun, snowflake, July morning, jack-o'-lantern.*

Traditional haiku is based in nature and uses strong, concrete nouns to paint a picture of what the poet has seen (or imagined).

Avoid nouns like *love, happiness,* or *peace,* which are ideas and concepts. Instead use concrete nouns like *lily pad, frog,* or *splash.*

The most important part of haiku is the contrast between two images. The images can be pictures, sounds, or words that describe any of the other senses. Look for two images that contradict each other in some way.

For example: *dry leaves in the corner of an empty pool* contrast *water* (now absent) and *dryness.*

Another example: *melted snow puddles* and *a robin on the fence* portray a change of seasons from winter to spring.

The surprise in haiku – sometimes called the Aha! Moment – is the connection the reader perceives between the images.

Here are some haiku examples written by poet Polly Swafford, a retired secondary social studies/English teacher:

first snowfall
one red mitten
under the swing

bright stars
carolers sing
at the mall

bedtime –
whippoorwill's call
floats through the window

black birds chatter
in the corn field
red leaves fall

first crocus
white squirrel
digs for acorns

soft snowflakes
fill backyard birdbath
cardinal waits

checking out
the Christmas tree
our new puppy

fat robin
atop sign post
two hour parking only

– haikus by Polly Swafford

⇨ **Try this!**

Think of two images that define the moment of change from one season to the next. Write a haiku.

THE I LOVE TO WRITE BOOK

Acrostic Poems

Here's another fun and easy way to write a poem called an *acrostic.*

Choose a word (or even a name) for the title. Then, write the same word in a vertical line under the title.

Below is a poem named "Winter." The first letter of each line of the poem spells out the title: W-I-N-T-E-R.

Choose your own title for a poem. Use each letter as the first letter of a word in a phrase . . . that tells something about the title.

There's your poem!

Winter

Wacky weather
Icicles are melting
Never warm
Toes are frozen
Everyone wants the sun
Red cheeks

> *– Clayton Phillips, 3rd grade*

 **Try this!**

Write an acrostic poem.

Title of the Poem: _____

Letter ___ _____

Letter ___ _____

Letter ___ _____

Letter ___ _____

Letter ___ _____

Letter ___ _____

Letter ___ _____

Letter ___ _____

Apology Poems

Have you ever done something that you know you should be sorry for . . . but you'd do it again in a heartbeat? In fact, you're not sorry at all?

That is the basis of an "apology poem," written in the style of a famous American poet, William Carlos Williams.

William Carlos Williams invented this type of poem when he wrote a poem called "This Is Just to Say." The poem speaks to a "victim" of the narrator's action.

> "It is not what you say that matters but the manner in which you say it; there lies the secret of the ages."
>
> William Carlos Williams (1883–1963), American poet

The first lines of an apology poem say what the poet (or the imaginary narrator) did. The next lines tell why it matters. Then, an apology stands alone on its own line (something like "I'm sorry" or "forgive me"). And, in this style, after the apology, the poet makes a statement that tells the reader the speaker is not sorry at all.

Notice that there is no *but* or *however* after the apology. The statement stands alone.

Here's an example. Can you see how the poem follows the apology poem structure? (Notice the line spaces between the elements of the poem.)

Dear Kellen (the "victim")

I stole your Gameboy (what I did)
that you really wanted to play (why it matters)

I'm sorry (an apology)

I beat the game
and the high score (why the poet is not sorry)

 – Harris Bailey, 6th grade

You can write an apology poem about something you did. Or you can make up something someone else did or a fictional character might have done.

(Poets often use a "narrator's voice" as the speaker in a poem.) Here's an example using a narrator's voice.

With Apologies to William Carlos Williams

I have stolen
the stars
that were once in the midnight sky

and which
you were probably
saving
for your dreams

Forgive me
they were so intriguing

so bright and so wishful.

– Harvir Sanghera, 10th grade

⇨ **Try this!**

Fill out this form. Arrange it as an apology poem.

1. Title (Who is the "victim" of the action?) _____

2. What happened? _____

3. Choose one: Forgive me / I'm sorry / I apologize _____

4. What was the result of what happened that makes the apology less than sincere?

_____

_____

Create Characters

A character is a person in your story. (The character may be an animal, a human, a robot, or a machine with personality.)

Your job as a writer is to introduce this character to your readers in a way that makes the character seem real and unforgettable.

You can do that by showing what the character does, what the character says, and what other people in the story say about him or her.

Here are a few examples:

What the character does:
> Chad moved his pawn in front of the opponent's queen on the chessboard.

What the character says:
> "I've been taking dancing lessons since second grade," Ali said.

What others say about the character:
> "Don't trust Joey," Ahmed said. "He stole my favorite CD."

▶ *Definition: Characterization*
Characterization is showing the reader what a character is like.

To develop a believable character, you must know much more about him or her than you show your reader. Before you start writing, develop a character sketch by answering questions about him or her.

On the next two pages you'll find a worksheet to get you started.

"There are things I know about many of the characters in the Harry books that might not make it into the books themselves . . . too much information, not enough space!"

J.K. Rowling (1965–), author of the Harry Potter series

Worksheet: Character Sketch

1. What is the character's name?

_____

2. Is it human?

_____

    a. If not, what is it? _____

    b. If so, is it a boy or girl? _____

3. How old is he/she?

_____

4. Describe his/her physical size, height, hair (color and style), and any disability (wears glasses, wears braces, uses a wheelchair).

_____

_____

_____

5. What is the character's occupation?

_____

6. How many brothers and sisters does he/she have?

_____

7. What is he/she wearing (when first met)?

_____

8. Describe his/her room by selecting objects that reveal information (a baseball trophy shows a talent for the sport, shelves full of books reveal the character likes to read):

_____

_____

_____

MARY-LANE KAMBERG

9. If the character is the "good guy," list three bad things about him or her. If the character is the "bad guy," list three good things about him or her.

_____

_____

_____

10. What is he/she good at?

_____

_____

11. What is he/she afraid of?

_____

12. What is he/she sorry about doing?

_____

13. What secrets does he/she keep?

_____

14. Who is the character's best friend?

_____

15. What does this character want?

_____

_____

Once you can answer these kinds of questions, you'll know how your characters will act in the different situations you put them in.

When you are creating characters, give them both good traits and bad traits, no matter whether you're creating the hero or the villain.

As your story develops, reveal as many items from your character sketch as you need. You don't need to use them all, but your readers need to know enough to decide how they feel about each character.

⇨ **Try this!**

Create a character sketch for every character in your story.

That way, you'll know how to make them real for your readers.

⇨ **Try this!**

Describe your pet by creating a character sketch.

Then, write one or two sentences . . . in a way to tell us something unusual about your pet that gives your pet a unique "character."

⇨ **Try this!**

Pretend you witnessed a man running away from a house that you later learned was robbed.

When the police interview you, describe the suspect.

What did he look like?

How tall? Fat or thin?

What color hair?

What was he wearing?

What did you notice that was unusual about him?

How did the suspect act?

Did you hear him speak?

What did he sound like?

What did he say?

Tell a Story

The best way to tell a story is whatever works.

What happens in a story (and the order it happens) is the *plot.* One way to tell a story dates to Aristotle's time, around 300 B.C.

Narrative form has three parts: a beginning, a middle, and an end. If you're writing fiction, each part of the story plays an important role in the whole.

You can also think of the beginning, middle, and end in terms of three ideas: character, conflict, and change.

"People are most deeply moved not by
the reaching of the goal
but by the grandness
of effort involved
in getting there –
or failing to get there."

Max Lerner (1902–1992),
Russian-born American journalist,
editor, and educator

▶ *Definition: Plot*
Plot is the story – what happens and the order it happens in.

The three parts of a story are not the same lengths. Because so much happens in the middle, that section is the longest part.

Here's what you need in each section of a story:

The Beginning (Character)

The Beginning introduces a character. In fact, the first person the reader meets is usually the *main* character. It is best to start "in the action," showing that character doing something or talking with someone.

The reader learns something the character is good at . . . and something he or she fears. Remember to *show* the character doing the thing he or she is good at and *show* the character reacting to the thing he or she fears. (Your writing will be stronger if you show than if you simply *tell* the reader: "Angie was a good cheerleader, but she was afraid of heights." Instead, think about ways to help the reader see that.)

To make a good story, the character needs a *problem.* The problem can be only one of two possibilities: either he or she wants something . . . or wants to keep something he or she has.

For instance, suppose your main character is the quarterback for the school football team. He might see a pretty girl and want to take her to the prom. Or in another story, a girl might want to find her long lost twin sister. In another, perhaps a girl wants to keep a wild mustang she found running loose on her parents' ranch.

The problem must be important to the character, because it will drive the story through to the end. Of course, the character may try to avoid dealing with the problem for a short while. But soon, the character begins a journey to get what he or she wants (or to keep what he or she has).

This is the end of the beginning.

▶ Definition: Obstacle
Something that stands between the character and what he or she wants or wants to keep. An obstacle can be another person, a machine, the weather, or even the character's own personality, character flaws, or disability.

The Middle (Conflict)
Trouble happens in the Middle of the story. As soon as the character tries to move toward the goal, something blocks the way.

Think about it: if the character immediately gets what he or she wants, there is no story. For a good story, something must be in the character's way – something that makes it difficult to reach the goal.

And it must be something that can't be easily fixed.

In a story, trouble is called *conflict.* (In real life, conflict is a bad thing. But in a story, it's a great way to create lots of interest!)

▶ Definition: Conflict
In a story, conflict is a way to create interest. Conflict happens when someone (or something) stands in a character's way and prevents him or her from easily getting what he or she wants.

The "villain" can be another person, a machine, the weather. Or even the character's own personality, character flaws, or disability can get in the way.

Not only does the character face a first obstacle, he or she faces three obstacles – one at a time. As the character tries to overcome each obstacle, he or she fails every time.

Each obstacle is more difficult than the one before it, and each failure results in more complications. Each failure puts him further from the goal.

The first time the character tries and fails, the reader might say, "Oh, no." The second time the character tries and fails, the reader might say, "OH! NO!" The third time he or she tries and fails, the reader might say, *"ALL IS LOST! EVERYTHING IS HOPELESS!"*

In narrative form, this hopeless point in the story is called the "dark moment." It seems that the character will never reach the goal. He won't get a date for the prom. She'll never find her sister. She will lose the wild mustang.

After the dark moment, the character tries one more time. This time he faces his greatest fear – the one you gave him in the beginning of the story, but now even bigger. If he was afraid of a garden snake in the beginning, for instance, now he faces a boa constrictor! If she was afraid of a teeny spider in the beginning, she now faces a huge tarantula!

▶ *Definition: Dark moment*
This is the point in a story when the character has failed to reach the goal or solve the problem for the third time, and all seems lost.

To face this final (and scariest) obstacle, the character uses something he or she is good at (whatever you showed the reader about the character in the beginning, so that inner strength or talent is not a complete surprise).

After this last conflict, the character either gets what he or she wants, or decides that the goal was wrong. (The character cannot just say he doesn't want it because he or she has failed. The character must come to realize that his or her goal was truly unworthy.)

For example, during his efforts to get a date with the popular girl, the character might learn that he doesn't like her and doesn't want to take her to the prom after all. In another story, based on what the character learns about her twin, she may decide the twin is better off living her life without knowing she has a sister. Or, the girl on the ranch might realize that her mustang will be happier running free in the canyon.

Either way, the character must solve the problem either by getting what he or she wants or coming to a realization that the goal was unworthy. And the character must solve the problem on his or her own. No one else can do it.

Now, you might think that winning (or losing) is the end of the story! In fact, the End (short, but sweet) has just begun.

The End (Change)

The End is where you wrap up all the details of the story. If you have raised questions in the readers' minds, this is where you answer them.

Most important, the reader discovers what the character has learned from his struggle against the obstacles.

What the character learns is something he or she shares with the other characters (but not in a preachy way), so they (and the reader) benefit from the experience. In the End, something has changed, and nothing will ever be the same.

⇨ Try this!

Cut out 15 pictures of people from old magazines. Put them in a pile. Next, cut out 15 pictures of objects. Put them in another pile.

Now, without looking, choose one person and one thing. Write a story about the character wanting the thing.

What can stand in the character's way?

Follow the narrative form described in this chapter.

Worksheet: 7 Steps to Story Success!

This worksheet will help you brainstorm . . . and work through the three main sections of a narrative story: Beginning, Middle, and End.

The Beginning (Character)

We meet the character and discover what he or she wants most of all and must try to get or achieve.

Step 1.
Who is the main character?

_____

What is he or she good at?

_____

What does he or she most fear?

_____

What happens to make the character want something, or want to keep something?

_____

What does he or she want?

_____

The Middle (Conflict)

This will be the longest part of the story.

Step 2.
What three obstacles get in the way?

a. _____

b. _____

c. _____

Step 3.
After the dark moment, what is the final obstacle?
(Hint: it should involve what the character most
fears – see Step 1.)

_____

_____

Step 4.
What talent that you gave the character in Step 1
does he/she use to overcome the final obstacle?

_____

_____

Step 5.
Does the character get what he or she wants (or
decide he or she doesn't want it after all)? Why?

_____

_____

The End (Change)
Short, but sweet!

Step 6.
What has the character learned? How has his or her
world forever changed?

_____

_____

Step 7.
Write the story! Use action and dialogue to move the
story along.

Revise, Edit, and Proofread

Rewrite, Rewrite, Rewrite

When you finish your first draft of a poem or story, your job as a "creative" writer is done.

But your job as an editor has just begun.

First drafts are never the best they can be. First drafts are where you search for the story you really want to tell. You get it down in bits and pieces.

Once you make it all the way through to the end of the poem, story, or essay, the rewriting begins: rearrange the paragraphs, delete some words and sentences, add new ones.

Start by reading the entire piece of writing. Have you chosen the best structure, words, spelling, grammar, and punctuation? Try to step away from your writing and read as if you were reading it for the first time.

Consider rewriting by examining your writing with the following ideas in mind:

"It is perfectly okay to write garbage – as long as you edit brilliantly."

C. J. Cherryh (1942–), American science-fiction and fantasy author; she began writing at the age of ten.

Rewrite for structure.

One way to rewrite is to check for the structure of the story or poem.

Have you used the best structure?

Is inverted pyramid best?

Or should you switch to narrative form?

Does your poem work best in rhyme, or should you try free verse?

▶ Definition: Structure

Structure is the skeleton of your writing, the order you use to show the reader what happens. In a report, for instance, the structure is the outline that shows the order you use to explain the topic.

Some other examples of structure for prose are narrative form (see "Tell a Story," page 97) and inverted pyramid (see "Report the News," page 63).

Examples of structure for poetry include haiku, acrostic poems, list poems, and apology poems.

Rewrite characters and details.

Is the right person telling the story? In a mystery, is the right character the bad guy?

In your poem, do you need that bowl of apples on that table? Or would a single apple in a lunchbox say more?

Rewrite for better use of language.

Get rid of places where you say the same thing twice. Add "color" words. See if you can use a simple word in place of a big word. Look for places to use dialogue. Add action.

Rewrite for spelling, grammar, and punctuation.

Make sure your reader understands what you are trying to say. The more you correct your own work, the better writer you'll become.

Read through your writing once again, this time with your pen or pencil in hand. As you read, make finishing touches.

When you make notes for corrections or ideas for improvements, use a different color ink from the one you used to write.

If you wrote on a computer, print out your story and work with a hard copy.

Use a dictionary to check your spelling. Use a thesaurus or synonym finder to learn new words for old thoughts.

MARY-LANE KAMBERG

➡️ **Try this!**

Every story has two sides (or more). Read a story that you or someone else wrote.

Rewrite it, but make a different character the hero. What would the new character think, say, and do? How would she describe what happens?

➡️ **Try this!**

Find a place in a book where characters are talking to each other.

Rewrite it so that each character says the exact opposite of what he or she said in the original.

➡️ **Try this!**

Read a story or poem that you have written before.

See if you can find any errors in spelling, grammar, or punctuation. If you do, rewrite it with the corrections.

"The best part of all, the absolutely most delicious part, is finishing it and then doing it over.

I rewrite a lot, over and over again, so that it looks like I never did."

Toni Morrison (1931–), American novelist and winner of the 1988 Pulitzer Prize for *Beloved*

Critique Checklist

If you want to evaluate someone else's work (or even your own!), this checklist will help you give constructive examples of where the author did a good job . . . and some places to suggest improvement.

Remember, a good critique also mentions good points, as well as places the work can be improved. It's always good to start, and end, with positive comments . . . . with your suggestions for improvements sandwiched in the middle.

_____ 1. Does the beginning capture your interest?

_____ 2. Do you like the main character? (Why or why not?)

_____ 3. Do you understand what the main character wants?

_____ 4. Are there specific places where you have suggestions for better words or ways to say something?

_____ 5. Is there any place where the author slipped and reminded you that you were reading a story instead of letting you stay "in the story" as a reader?

_____ 6. Is it too easy for the character to get what he/she wants?

_____ 7. Are there any words (like "tree") that can be made more specific (like "oak")?

_____ 8. Do you have any suggestions for improving the plot?

_____ 9. Is the ending satisfying?

_____ 10. Do you notice any grammar, punctuation, or spelling mistakes?

MARY-LANE KAMBERG

More Tips for Rewriting

As you write, use the following tips. When you rewrite, look at each item below and check your work against this list.

Remember, editing is a creative process in itself. Nothing is always right or always wrong. You can break any of the following "rules."

But most of the time, these suggestions make your writing better.

> "Books aren't written, they're rewritten…
> It is one of the hardest things to accept, especially after the seventh rewrite hasn't quite done it."
>
> Michael Crichton (1942–), American science-fiction novelist and author of *Jurassic Park*; he wrote his first play at the age of nine.

Use strong, specific nouns.

Use adjectives only now and then. An adjective may be a sign that you need a different noun.

Mark Twain, author of *The Adventures of Tom Sawyer,* said, "If you can catch an adjective, kill it." You can say *house* or *tree,* but *cottage* or *oak* are more specific, and therefore, stronger. (*Cottage* is also stronger than *little house,* which needs the adjective *little* to help it.)

Select which items you show the reader based on the mood of the character and items that will be important later in the story. For instance, if the hero defeats the villain in a boxing match at the end, show the reader the boxing gloves early in the story – before the character needs them. If you forgot to do that in your first draft, go back to the beginning of the story and find a place to slip them in.

Use strong, specific verbs. Use adverbs only now and then.

An "action" word is stronger than a "being" word. *He ran* is stronger than *he was running.*

He sat is stronger than *he is sitting.*

He plopped into the chair is stronger than *he sat.*

Avoid words that end in *-ly.* Instead of saying *she went slowly down the stairs,* say: *she crept down the stairs.*

The frequent use of "and" may mean you need a new sentence.

Example:

> She ran into the house and slipped on the wet
> kitchen floor and skidded into the stepladder and
> paint spilled all over.

Better:

> She ran into the house and slipped on the wet
> kitchen floor. She skidded into the stepladder.
> Paint spilled all over.

Look for places where characters can move or speak to each other.

Tell your story through action and dialogue.

Example:

> Her father scolded her for running. She said she was
> sorry.

Better:

> She ran into the house.
>   "Slow down!" Dad shouted.
>   She stopped in the hall. "I'm sorry."

Avoid words that end in -ing.

Crossing the street, the lawn sprinkler got his new suit wet . . .means that the *lawn sprinkler* is crossing the street, not the character!

Also, If you use an *-ing* word to connect two actions, be sure the character can do both at the same time! *Getting out of the truck, he opened the screen door* is impossible . . . unless the truck is parked on the front porch. Instead say: *He got out of the truck. On the front porch, he opened the screen door.*

Use all the senses.

Especially in poems and stories, but also in essays or reports, use sights, smells, sounds, tastes and textures to make your writing come alive and define the special world you create.

MARY-LANE KAMBERG

Use "bad" heroes and "good" villains.

Give your hero some faults. Give your villain some good qualities.

That way, your characters will be more realistic, and your story will be less predictable and more interesting.

Make your characters do things ... not "begin" to do things.

Example:
```
The students started to laugh.
```

Better:
```
The students laughed.
```

Use *began to* . . . only if the action is going to stop and you want to focus on that:

```
He started to laugh, but noticed his sister crying.
```

Say things only once.

If you show readers that a character has blond hair, you don't need to keep reminding them *every* time you show that character. If you say he is an orphan, you don't have to say his mother and father died.

Also, leave out descriptive words that repeat meaning.

If someone *stands,* you don't need to add *up.*

When you say *skunk,* you don't need *black and white.* The fur colors are already included in the meaning of the word.

Show, don't tell.

Pretend your characters are actors on a stage. (They are!)

Instead of telling the audience that someone is nervous, show it by portraying something the character does . . . in a nervous way.

Let your readers figure out how the character feels.

If you use an adjective to describe *how* a character feels, you're not showing but telling.

Instead of using an adjective, a better way is to rewrite the sentence or sentences to show the character in action instead.

Example:
`Mary is nervous.`

Better:
`Mary fidgeted with her car keys.`

Avoid prepositional phrases that start with "of."

Find another way to say what you mean. In the example below, *of murder* in the first version is a prepositional phrase. In the improved version, the editor shortened it for a stronger impact.

Example:
`The detective investigated a case of murder.`

Better:
`The detective investigated a murder case.`

Here are some more examples:

Example: *the title of the book is . . .*
Better: *the book title is . . .*

Example: *the heart of a lion*
Better: *a lion's heart*

No, you don't have to change all prepositional phrases. Sometimes, they add necessary meaning.

However, when you find yourself using one, take an extra look to see if you've used the best word choices or word order.

(Note: in addition to phrases that begin with *of,* watch for those that start with *at, for,* and *from.)*

Use active voice.

Make characters act instead of having actions done to them.

Passive voice:
```
Torin was hit by Becky.
```

Active voice:
```
Becky hit Torin.
```

Avoid "detached body parts"!

Watch for body parts that have become detached from their body!

For example, *her hands held the baby* . . . brings an odd image of two hands floating in the air.

Their eyes met . . . brings a picture of bouncing eyeballs introducing themselves to each other.

Instead say: *She held the baby* . . . or *Her gaze met his.*

✔ Writing Tip

Your writing will be strong and interesting if you make every word count. That means each word must do an important job. If you don't need it, delete it.

⇨ Try this!

First, take the quick "Tighten Your Writing" quiz on the following page. Then, check your answers (see pages 127–28).

Now, take something you have written. See how many of the tips to tighten your writing you can use in your own work.

Rewrite places where you "broke the rules."

(Note: you are still the writer! You don't have to obey every single rule every time. But in general, try to follow them . . . unless you have a good reason to break them.)

Quiz: Tighten Your Writing!

Look at the following sentences created by poet and editor Terry Hoyland (reprinted by permission). Revise them to be clearer, less wordy, or less repetitious.

Pretend you are an editor. Write a revision of each sentence. (Then, compare your edits with suggested revisions on pages 127–28.)

1. The President will not make any changes in policy, at this point in time.

2. "At the present time, we are experiencing precipitation," Katie said.

3. A border of yellow daffodils surrounded the rose garden.

4. John clenched his teeth tightly.

5. The big, gorgeous, slow-moving, blue and gold blimp flew over Arrowhead Stadium during the game.

6. "He is a personal friend of mine," I said to the policeman.

7. "He was hit by Joe."

8. A widow lady dug in the brown dirt beside the statue.

MARY-LANE KAMBERG

Let Your Computer Help You

For quick editing, use tools in your word-processing program to fix obvious errors.

Run the "Spell Check" and "Find" (or "Search") functions (see tips below).

But don't rely on them to be perfect. Spell Check catches *misspelled* words, but not words you've used in the wrong places.

For example, if you meant to write *cars* but typed *care*, Spell Check will skip right over it. That's because *care* is a correctly spelled word.

It just wasn't the right word!

So, after using Spell Check and fixing anything it catches, you still want to reread your work to be sure you said what you meant to say.

When in doubt, follow Thomas Jefferson's advice, "Take care that you never spell a word wrong. Always before you write a word, consider how it is spelled, and, if you do not remember, turn to a dictionary."

> "Writing is rewriting.
>
> A writer must learn to deepen characters, trim writing, intensify scenes.
>
> To fall in love with a first draft to the point where one cannot change it is to greatly enhance the prospects of never publishing."
>
> **Richard North Patterson (1947–), bestselling American novelist**

Find or Search function

Another computer tool that helps writers edit is the Find function, sometimes called Search. With it, you can quickly search your piece of writing for words (or even parts of words) that are the most important to double-check.

Use the Find function to locate some or all of the words (or letter-combinations) listed on the next page. For example, searching for *ly* will locate, one by one, each word ending in *-ly)*.

```
ly
ing
is
was
are
were
has
have
had
began to (or started to)
of
and
very
that
```

Why check for these? These words and letter-combinations are signs of potential weak spots in your writing.

Take a good, hard look at each one the computer finds. (You might mark them as you go on a hard copy, then review them.) You don't have to change every one, but in general, try to improve the sentence it is in.

Note: when you use the Find function, you enter the word (or letter-combination), then click something like Find Next. It takes you to the first case it finds. Then, clicking Find Next takes you to the next.

You can quickly work through your document.

As you use this tool, your writing will quickly improve, and you will soon be checking and fixing these problems on your own as you write. After a while, you may not need to search for every word on this list . . . just the ones that you know are still giving you trouble.

 Try this!

Take a piece of your writing and use the computer's Find or Search function to find all adverbs you've used that end in -ly.

Now, see how many you can delete . . . if you choose a different, stronger verb that doesn't need that adverb!

Share Your Work

Writing is meant to be read. So, if you've never shared your work with others, now's the time to start!

Show your poem or story to a teacher, librarian, or a friend who writes. Ask for feedback on what they like about your writing and how you can improve it.

Listen to their advice and make the revisions that you agree with. (No matter what others think, the writing is always *your* piece of work, and you must make final decisions about changes.)

After proofreading the final copy, send it out. School newspapers and literary magazines, organization newsletters, local newspapers, magazines, online publications, and other media stand ready to publish your writing.

"A writer's duty is to register what it is like for him or her to be in the world."

Zadie Smith (1975–), British novelist

✔ Writing Tip

A writers critique club is a great way to share your work with others. If you don't have one, start one!

Ask a teacher or librarian to help you find other writers in your school, and pick a place and time to meet regularly.

Read your work and listen to others'.

When you talk about someone else's work, follow this advice from children's writer Wilma Yeo: "Tell the truth, but be kind." First, talk about the parts you liked best. Then tell parts that confused you or reminded you that you were reading a story instead of being "in the story."

End with another positive comment.

What manuscripts look like

Print your manuscript on plain white, 20-pound, 8½" x 11" paper. (Editors do not like to get submissions on colored paper.)

Poems (just put one poem on each page) may be single-spaced. But all "prose" (regular text, like this paragraph you're reading now) must be double-spaced. (It won't end up that way, but it's how editors need to see your writing; it allows them to make notes in between the lines).

If you don't have access to a computer, many places that publish work by young writers accept handwritten manuscripts if you write neatly. Include illustrations only if the publication asks for them.

In the top left-hand corner, single-space your name, address, phone number, and e-mail address (yours or a parent's; for more on e-mail advice, see "Tips for Success," page 121).

Number the pages in the top right-hand corner.

On page 1, center the title about half-way down on the page. Double-space and type "By [YOUR NAME]." Triple-space, then start your story on that first page. Use 12-point Times New Roman or Courier font.

▶ *Definition: Manuscript*
A typed, printed, or handwritten version of a book, story, poem, or other piece of writing . . . before it is published.

Before sending in your work, become familiar with the publication you plan to send it to. If possible, read several copies. Or visit the publication's website and read a sample copy there. Why? Reading the publication gives you an idea of the kind of work editors select. That way, you can send something that "fits."

An important way to increase your chance of acceptance is to read and follow the submission guidelines. You can find them on the publication's website, or send a letter or e-mail to the editor asking for them.

Whenever you contact an editor by mail – to request guidelines or submit your work – include a self-addressed, stamped envelope (SASE). You may see the abbreviation SASE included in the guidelines, or you might not. Unless the publication specifically says "no SASE," always send one.

▶ *Definition: Submission guidelines*
A list of rules for sending your work to a publication.

MARY-LANE KAMBERG

► *Definition: SASE*
An SASE is a "Self-Addressed, Stamped Envelope."

To mail in a submission, place your manuscript in a 9" x 12" envelope. Enclose the SASE.

Write a brief "cover letter" (see next page) to the publication's editor. (The cover letter "covers" the manuscript in the envelope.) It includes your contact information, the title of your piece, and what type of writing it is: poem, short story, personal essay, etc.

► *Definition: Cover letter*
This is a brief letter that "covers" a manuscript submitted to a publication. It will be the first thing an editor sees.

When you start sending out your work, keep a manuscript log. Get a special notebook just for this purpose. Make columns to record the date, name of publication, and the title of the work you send.

Leave two blanks where you can record the response (accepted? rejected?) from the editor and the date he/she replied.

For example:

Manuscript Log

DATE	PUB NAME	TITLE OF PIECE	RESPONSE & DATE	
11/12	Launch Pad	"My Grandmother"	_____	____
12/3	Magic Dragon	"Magic Kingdom"	_____	____
12/11	The Acorn	"How To Wash a Dog"	_____	____

When the editor replies, write accepted or rejected and the date. This record will help you track where your work is and how long it takes to hear from an editor.

That way, the next time you send to that publication, you'll have a good idea how long you can expect to wait for a response. (Note: if you don't send an SASE, you won't get a reply.)

Sample: Cover Letter

Mary Smith
1234 E. First Street
Overland Park, KS 66212

September 3, 2009

Mr. Phil Jones
Kids Magazine
5678 W. Second Street
Kansas City, MO 64111

Dear Mr. Jones:

Please consider the enclosed story "Softball Adventure" for publication in the "Written by Kids" section of *Kids Magazine*.

I am in the 8th grade at Oxford Middle School and have been writing since I was in 3rd grade.

I enclose an SASE, and I look forward to hearing from you.

Thank you for your consideration.

Sincerely,

[your signature]

Mary Smith

Acceptances & Rejections

Hooray! Your work has been accepted.

If your submitted piece is good and fits what an editor wants, you may get a letter, an e-mail, or even a phone call from the editor saying they want to publish your story, poem, or article.

You may be asked to sign a contract, usually just to give them the okay to include your work in their publication. (In most cases, you still "own" the piece.)

Or possibly you signed a form when you first submitted a piece; this might have been part of a contest entry form, for instance, okaying in advance that they could publish the work if it got an award.

Either way, if you're younger than 18, you'll need your parents to sign as well.

The editor may even offer to pay you money. Or, common for small publications, he/she might just offer several free copies of the issue your work appears in. (If there is no such offer, ask about payment in cash – or request copies of the publication so you can save a good copy and possibly give extra copies away to friends or relatives.)

> "I endured two years of rejections, and I really think determination is every bit as important as talent, so don't give up!"
>
> Judy Blume (1938–), American author of many award-winning novels for children and young adults

✔ Writing Tip

Never pay a publisher to publish your work.
Reputable magazines never ask for payment.
Also, beware of book publishers who offer to sell you an expensive book where your work appears. Say, "Thanks, but no thanks!"
However, if your work appears in a legitimate book or magazine, you may be eligible to buy extra copies at a discount. Ask!

Publishing usually takes a long time, so be patient waiting for a copy of your work in print. When you get it, share your success! Make photocopies for friends, relatives, teachers, and your school librarian. Also make a special binder or scrapbook to keep all your published work.

And send more of your work to the same publisher, as well as to other magazines or online journals.

Rejection

If you receive a rejection slip saying the publication can't use your work, take heart. The rejection may have nothing to do with the quality of your writing. Rejection is common even to expert writers.

Remember, the editor is rejecting *only* this particular piece of writing – not you as a writer, and certainly not you as a person.

Here are some reasons why work gets rejected:

- ▶ the publication recently published a similar piece
- ▶ the author failed to read and follow submission guidelines
- ▶ the topic is wrong for the readership
- ▶ the publication has already accepted enough stories or poems
- ▶ the editor likes your writing, but not this particular poem or story

Look at the rejection as a chance to send your work now to a different magazine. The more work you send out, the better your chances of getting published. Good writers get rejections; it's part of the game!

Most important: never give up. Keep writing and sending out your work.

 Try this!

See the next chapter ("Where to Submit Your Work for Publication") for a list of places that publish work by young writers. Find and study the guidelines for one of the publications listed there.

Read a few examples of the writing they publish.

Then, choose one of your poems or stories that you feel best fits the publication. Send it in!

MARY-LANE KAMBERG

Where To Submit Your Work for Publication

The following list includes print and online publications that publish work by young writers.

Before sending your work, read at least one issue of the magazine – either in hard copy or online.

Then, to submit a piece, go to the magazine's website for submission guidelines for young writers.

Or e-mail or write a letter, saying: "Please send me your submission guide-lines for young writers." Include your name, address, phone number, and e-mail address (yours or a parent's or teacher's e-mail; see tips below). If by mail, enclose a stamped, self-addressed envelope for the editor's reply.

When sending your work, never submit your only copy! Make a photocopy or print an extra copy from your computer.

For more print and online publishers, ask a teacher or librarian, or search online for terms like "written by children" or "young writers."

> "Write as often as possible, not with the idea at once of getting into print, but as if you were learning an instrument."
>
> **J. B. Priestley (1894–1984), British novelist, playwright, and radio commentator**

Tips for success

For professional success and personal safety, always use courtesy, common sense, and (if using e-mail) caution in any correspondence:

1. Check out the publication to be sure it's "real" and legitimate. Look for it online or in a bookstore. Look it up in a reference book of magazine listings, such as *Writer's Market;* ask for help with this at the reference desk of your public library.

2. Some contests are free. Others charge $5–$15. Be wary of con-tests that charge more or have hidden catches. For more, see this warning about contest scams: www.sfwa.org/Beware/contests.html.

3. Let a parent, or a teacher or responsible adult, know what you are submitting and the name of the magazine. You might even ask an adult

to send it in for you (some places require this), using his or her e-mail address instead of yours (if submitting work online) . . . or even if just requesting information.

4. Be careful what you submit. You might feel some personal stories must be written, including subjects that you have trouble dealing with, like grief, hurt feelings, or other pain. But not all stories should be published in magazines for kids. (Save them for later, though. When you are an adult, you can decide if you want to share those stories with the world.)

5. Always be courteous. And in all cases, the correspondence should be only "business" and never "personal." If something seems odd to you, share your question with a parent or teacher.

Print Magazines

Creative Kids

This magazine publishes games, stories, and opinions by and for writers ages 8–14. Editors are looking for original cartoons, songs, stories (500 to 1,200 words), puzzles, editorials, poetry, and plays. Work can be submitted by the author or by parent or teacher. Include SASE. Send to: *Creative Kids*, Submissions Editor, PO Box 8813, Waco, TX 76714. See guidelines at www.prufrock.com. (Click on "Submissions Guidelines" on the home page.)

Magic Dragon

This quarterly magazine publishes writing and art by children in elementary school grades. Editors are looking for stories and essays (fiction or nonfiction, up to three pages), and poetry (up to 30 lines). Their website is www.magicdragonmagazine.com. Writing may be submitted by e-mail to info@magicdragonmagazine.com. All submissions must also attach a Permission to Publish form (available on their website; go to home page, click on "Send Work" and you will then see the link to that form near the bottom of that page of submission info). Or mail to Magic Dragon, PO Box 687, Webster, NY 14580.

MARY-LANE KAMBERG

New Moon

Subtitle: *The Magazine for Girls and Their Dreams*

This magazine uses fiction, nonfiction, poetry, reviews of books with strong girl characters or written by women, articles about historical women and girls, and letters by girls ages 8–14. Editors are especially interested in activists and adventurers and such topics as prejudice, equality, and current controversy. For a good example of an online safety policy, see www.newmoon.org/safety; *New Moon* works to create safe, supportive communities for their contributors. Submission guidelines, themes, and deadlines are posted at www.newmoon.org; click on *New Moon Magazine,* then "submissions." Send to: *New Moon,* 2 W First Street, #101, Duluth, MN 55802.

Skipping Stones

This multi-cultural children's magazine seeks original artwork, photos, stories, pen pal letters, recipes, cultural celebrations, songs, games, book reviews, and writings about culture, religion, interests and experiences, all by young writers ages 7–18. Send to: *Skipping Stones,* PO Box 3939, Eugene, OR 97403. Check for submission guidelines at www.skippingstones.org.

Stone Soup

Writers up to age 13 may submit stories, poems, and book reviews. Include your name, age, home address, phone number, and e-mail address if you have one. Please do not include a self-addressed stamped envelope. They do not accept e-mail submissions. "We like to think that serious young authors would be more than willing to polish their work, print it out in a nice format, and mail it to us." Send to: *Stone Soup,* Submissions Dept., PO Box 83, Santa Cruz, CA 95063. Their website is www.stonesoup.com.

Teen Ink

This monthly print magazine, written by teens for teens, also has a website with more than 18,000 pages of student writing. Writers must be between the ages of 13 and 19. Categories include art, poetry, fiction, nonfiction, opinion, reviews, and more. Title all work, and label it fiction or nonfiction. Include your name, year of birth, home address/city/state/ZIP code, telephone number, and the names of your school and English teacher on each submission. Send holiday-theme pieces at least two months early. Include SASE. Mail to *Teen Ink,* Box 30, Newton, MA 02461. Submission guidelines at www.teenink.com/submissions.

Online Publications

Cyberteens

This website seeks original poetry, fiction, and nonfiction submissions on any subject appropriate for teens, written by teens. Paste your submission text into the body of your message and e-mail it to: editor@cyberteens.com. Include your name, age, and country. See guidelines at www.cyberteens.com (click from home page on "About Us," then on the next page, click on "Contact Us" to find the guidelines) .

Launch Pad Magazine

Subtitle: *Where Young Authors and Illustrators Take Off!*
This online magazine publishes fiction, nonfiction, poetry, book reviews, and artwork written and created by children ages 6–12. Sample topics include animals, fairy tales and fantasy, heroes, mysteries, the ocean, and sports. "Please review the submission guidelines with an adult before submitting." Send submissions to: *Launch Pad,* PO Box 80578, Baton Rouge, LA 70898, or e-mail editor@launchpadmag.com. See guidelines at www.launchpadmag.com.

Teen Voices Online

Teen Voices seeks "to further social and economic justice by empowering teenage and young adult women." It has two magazines: *Teen Voices* and *Teen Voices Online*. Girls ages 13–19 can submit writing, or a description of their activism. Use the form available online at www.teenvoices.com (from home page, click on "About *Teen Voices,*" then on "Get Involved," then on "Get Published"). Or mail it with a copy of the form to *Teen Voices Online,* PO Box 120027, Boston, MA 02112.

MARY-LANE KAMBERG

Appendix I
Additional Resources

You mostly teach yourself to write . . . by writing. And by reading books for fun.

But you can also learn to improve your writing by reading books and magazines *about* writing, and much information is available online.

Here are some recommended resources:

> "A good writer is forever a student of writing."
>
> Donald Morrison Murray (1924– 2006), columnist for the *Boston Globe*

Books

A Beginning, a Muddle, and an End, by Avi
Bird by Bird: Some Instructions on Writing and Life, by Anne Lamott
The Elements of Style, by William Strunk, Jr. and E. B. White
On Writing Well, by William Zinsser
The Poetry Home Repair Manual, by Ted Kooser
Time for Kids: Ready, Set, Write! (A Writer's Handbook for School and Home), by the editors of *Time for Kids Magazine*
R is for Rhyme, by Judy Young
Writing Down the Bones, by Natalie Goldberg

Print magazines

Writing for Teens (Weekly Reader Publishing)
The Writer
Writer's Digest
Writers' Journal

Online resources

www.kristinegeorge.com
This website by children's writer Kristine George offers young writers great tips on such topics as observation and coming up with ideas for writing. Click on "For Students." Scroll down to "Tips for Poets."

www.pw.org
Sponsored by *Poets and Writers Magazine;* click on "Links." Click on "Young Writers Resources."

www.thescriptorium.net/youth.html
This virtual room for writers has a message board and writing tips; click on "Young Writers" for a young writers' webzine.

www.starrigger.net
Tips for aspiring writers from science fiction author Jeffrey A. Carver.

www.suemacy.com
Sue Macy's website; click on "For Kids" for 10 tips for young writers.

www.willamettewriters.com
A website with helpful writing tips, sponsored by the Willamette Writers, an Oregon writers organization. Click on "Young Willamette Writers."

youngwriter.org
This website is sponsored by *Young Writer,* "the magazine for children with something to say," based in the United Kingdom.

www.elizabethwinthrop.com
Elizabeth Winthrop's website has advice for young writers.

More information

www.lovetowritebook.org
For more, visit the website for *The I Love to Write Book,* to find basic information, advanced tips, a place to ask questions about anything in this book and other writing topics, success stories of young writers like you, interviews about writing (with some of your favorite writers) . . . plus the occasional contest and other fun stuff!

Appendix 2
Answers for Activities

Answers to quiz, page 17:

Police officer, F

Senator, H

Fire marshal, G

Business owner, C

Lawyer, D

Sales manager, E

Medical examiner, I

Scientist, B

Parent, A

Answers to "Tighten Your Writing!" quiz, page 112:

Here are suggested ways to edit the following sentences.

1. The President will not make any changes in policy, at this point in time.

   Better: *The President will make no changes in policy.*

   Explanation: Instead of using *not,* say things in a positive way. *At this point in time* adds nothing to the sentence. *Now* is already assumed; if the President makes changes in policy later, you can report it then.

2. "At the present time, we are experiencing precipitation," Katie said.

   Better: *"It's raining," Katie said.*

   Explanation: As in number 1 above, *now* is already assumed. *Experiencing precipitation* uses ten syllables to say something that you can say in three.

3. A border of yellow daffodils surrounded the rose garden.

   Better: *Daffodils bordered the rose garden.*

   Explanation: *Border* already means *surrounded,* so you don't need both words. (Note: you could say *the rose garden was bordered by daffodils,* but that sentence uses passive voice. Using active voice is better – most of the time.) Almost all daffodils are yellow, so you need to mention color only if the variety differs from the most common.

4. John clenched his teeth tightly.
   Better: *John clenched his teeth.*
   Explanation: *Clenched* already means tightly.

5. The big, gorgeous, slow-moving, blue and gold blimp flew over Arrowhead Stadium during the game.
   Better: *The blue and gold blimp flew over Arrowhead Stadium during the game.*
   Explanation: All blimps are big and slow moving, so you don't need those adjectives. (Remember: Mark Twain said to kill them!) *Gorgeous* is an author's opinion – some readers might think it's ugly. However, one good use of adjectives is to identify color.

6. "He is a personal friend of mine," I said to the policeman.
   Better: *"He's my friend," I told the policeman.*
   Explanation: Most people use contractions when they speak, so change *He is* to *He's* for a more conversational tone. *Of mine* uses two words to say the same thing as *my*. And *friend* already means *personal*. Finally, *said to* uses two words, while *told* is only one.

7. "He was hit by Joe."
   Better: *Joe hit him.*
   Explanation: Most of the time, let the subject of the sentence do the action; this is called active voice. (The first sentence above is in passive voice.)

8. A widow lady dug in the brown dirt beside the statue.
   Better: *A widow dug in the dirt beside the statue.*
   Explanation: All widows are women. (Men who have lost a spouse are called widowers.) Most dirt is brown, so you don't need to mention the color – unless your setting is in Oklahoma, where the dirt has a reddish tint, or somewhere else where dirt is an unusual color.

MARY-LANE KAMBERG

Glossary

Characterization   showing the reader what a character is like

Concrete noun   the name of a person, place or thing that you can see, hear, taste, touch, or smell

Conflict   In a story, a good way to create interest, created when someone (or something) stands in a character's way and prevents him or her from easily getting what he or she wants.

Copy   (used as a noun) the written words, or text, of an advertisement, news story, or magazine article

Copyright   legal protection for authors that prohibits others from copying their work without permission; it applies to books, poems, newspaper and magazine articles, songs, movie scripts, photographs, and other creative work.

Cover letter   a brief letter that "covers" a manuscript submitted to a publication

Dark moment   the point in a story told using narrative form when the character has failed to reach the goal or solve the problem for the third time, and all seems lost.

Dialogue   conversation between two or more people or characters

Feature story   a human-interest article in a newspaper or magazine

5 Ws and the H   the answers to who, what, when, where, why, and how; key elements of a news story (and often found in the first paragraph)

Free verse   poetry without end rhyme or formal rhythm

Genre   the category a work falls into (such as novel, poem, or essay, also more specific categories like mystery, comedy, Western, science fiction, or horror).

Haiku   a Japanese poetry form without a title that usually has three lines, a seasonal reference, and two contrasting images

Inverted pyramid   a story order, used in news reporting, with a broad summary in the first paragraph, followed by information decreasing in interest or importance

Keyword slugline   in the news industry, a line stating the subject of a story or letter to the editor. (According to the Associated Press, a keyword slugline should have no more than 21 letters.)

Lead   see *opening lead.*

Manuscript   a typed, printed, or handwritten version of a book, story, poem, or other piece of writing, before it is published

Metaphor   comparison of two unlike things that declares that one *is* the other

Noun   a word that is the name of a person, place, or thing

Obituary   a death notice published in a newspaper, magazine, or online; it usually includes a brief biography

Obstacle   something that stands between the main character and what he or she wants or wants to keep; it can be another person, a machine, the weather, or even the character's own personality, character flaws, or disability

Opening lead   the beginning of a news or feature story

MARY-LANE KAMBERG

Plot   the story – what happens in what order

Rejection slip   a postcard, note, or letter from an editor saying the publication can't use your work

Research   looking for information from other people, books, or the Internet or using your own observations

Rhyme   repetition of the ending sounds of words or lines of poetry

SASE   a Self-Addressed, Stamped Envelope

Simile   comparison of two unlike things, linked by *like* or *as*

Structure   the skeleton of a piece of writing, the order you use to you show the reader what happens

Submission guidelines   a list of rules for sending (submitting) your work to a publication

Index

MARY-LANE KAMBERG

About the Author

Mary-Lane Kamberg is an award-winning professional writer and speaker who founded and directs the Kansas City Writers Group's Young Writers Camp.

At the age of seven, she used her birthday money to buy a toy printing press. She went door to door asking neighbors if they had any news and published one issue of a neighborhood newspaper, which she sold for 2 cents each. At nine, she earned $1 for her first published poem. She wrote pep-club skits and worked on the school newspaper and literary journal.

But she never thought of herself as a writer until she was in college. She was reading a well-written article in *Time* magazine and thought: *Writing! That's what I want to do!*

She has a bachelor's degree in journalism from the William Allen White School of Journalism at the University of Kansas and has published 11 books, including two books for young readers, *Bono: Fighting World Hunger and Poverty* (Rosen Publishing, 2008) and *The "I Don't Know How To Cook" Book* (Adams Media Corp. 2004). She has also published hundreds of articles, short stories, and poems.

"If you wish to be a writer, write."

Epictetus, (55–135 A.D.),
Greek philosopher